Utilize este código QR para se cadastrar de forma mais rápida:

Ou, se preferir, entre em:
www.richmond.com.br/ac/livroportal

e siga as instruções para ter acesso aos conteúdos exclusivos do
Portal e Livro Digital

CÓDIGO DE ACESSO:

A 00003 PEACE2E 1 81186

Faça apenas um cadastro. Ele será válido para:

Da semente ao livro, sustentabilidade por todo o caminho

Plantar florestas
A madeira que serve de matéria-prima para nosso papel vem de plantio renovável, ou seja, não é fruto de desmatamento. Essa prática gera milhares de empregos para agricultores e ajuda a recuperar áreas ambientais degradadas.

Fabricar papel e imprimir livros
Toda a cadeia produtiva do papel, desde a produção de celulose até a encadernação do livro, é certificada, cumprindo padrões internacionais de processamento sustentável e boas práticas ambientais.

Criar conteúdos
Os profissionais envolvidos na elaboração de nossas soluções educacionais buscam uma educação para a vida pautada por curadoria editorial, diversidade de olhares e responsabilidade socioambiental.

Construir projetos de vida
Oferecer uma solução educacional Moderna é um ato de comprometimento com o futuro das novas gerações, possibilitando uma relação de parceria entre escolas e famílias na missão de educar!

Fotografe o Código QR e conheça melhor esse caminho.
Saiba mais em *moderna.com.br/sustentavel*

Students for
PEACE

Eduardo Amos
Renata Condi

1

Student's Book &
Workbook

Richmond

Richmond

Direção editorial: Sandra Possas

Edição executiva de inglês: Izaura Valverde
Edição executiva de produção e multimídia: Adriana Pedro de Almeida

Coordenação de arte: Raquel Buim
Coordenação de revisão: Rafael Spigel

Edição de texto: Ludmila De Nardi, Nathália Horvath, Wilson Chequi
Assistência editorial: Angela Cristina Costa Neves, Cíntia Afarelli Pereira, Leila Scatena
Elaboração de conteúdo: Beatriz Nosé, Christiane Araújo, Cristina Mayer, Doris Soares, Nathália R. S. Polachini, Paulo Machado
Preparação de originais: Helaine Albuquerque, Roberta Moratto Risther
Revisão: Carolina Waideman, Flora Manzione, Gabriele Martin Cândido, Gislaine Caprioli Costa, Kandy Saraiva, Katia Gouveia Vitale, Márcia Suzumura, Márcio Martins, Maria Luisa Prandina Rodrigues, Marina de Andrade, Vivian Cristina de Souza

Projeto gráfico: Carol Duran
Edição de arte: Carol Duran
Diagramação: Anexo Produção Editorial
Capa: Carol Duran
Criações: Anderson Sunakozawa, Carol Duran, Mateus Banti, Raquel Coelho
Ilustrações: Eduardo Medeiros, Estúdio Lab 307
Cartografia: Anderson de Andrade Pimentel

Website: Daniela Carrete, Frodo Almeida (*design*)
Social Media: Ana Paula Campos, Priscila Oliveira Vieira (edição de conteúdo); Eloah Cristina (analista de projetos); Altair Sampaio, Frodo Almeida (*design*)
Digital Hub: Ana Paula Campos, Priscila Oliveira Vieira (edição de conteúdo); Eloah Cristina (analista de projetos); Daniela Carrete (*design*)
PEACE Builders: Ana Paula Campos (edição de conteúdo); Daniela Carrete (*design*)
Digital Academy: Gabrielle Navarro, Thaís Teixeira Tardivo (edição de conteúdo); Daniel Favalli (coordenação de produção); Angela Urbinatti, Mônica M. Oldrine (*design*)
Novo Portal Educacional Richmond: Sheila Rizzi (edição)
Livro Digital Interativo: Gabrielle Navarro, Thaís Teixeira Tardivo (edição de conteúdo); Daniel Favalli (coordenação de produção); Angela Urbinatti (*design*)

Iconografia: Marcia Sato, Sara Alencar
Coordenação de *bureau*: Rubens M. Rodrigues
Tratamento de imagens: Fernando Bertolo, Joel Aparecido, Luiz Carlos Costa, Marina M. Buzzinaro
Pré-impressão: Alexandre Petreca, Everton L. de Oliveira, Márcio H. Kamoto, Vitória Sousa
Áudio: Maximal Studio

Todos os *sites* mencionados nesta obra foram reproduzidos apenas para fins didáticos. A Richmond não tem controle sobre seu conteúdo, o qual foi cuidadosamente verificado antes de sua utilização.
Websites mentioned in this material were quoted for didactic purposes only. Richmond has no control over their content and urges care when using them.
Embora todas as medidas tenham sido tomadas para identificar e contatar os detentores de direitos autorais sobre os materiais reproduzidos nesta obra, isso nem sempre foi possível. A editora estará pronta a retificar quaisquer erros dessa natureza assim que notificada.
Every effort has been made to trace the copyright holders, but if any omission can be rectified, the publishers will be pleased to make the necessary arrangements.

Impressão e acabamento: Coan Indústria Gráfica Ltda.
Lote: 284778 / 284779

Dados Internacionais de Catalogação na Publicação (CIP)
(Câmara Brasileira do Livro, SP, Brasil)

Amos, Eduardo
Students for peace / Eduardo Amos, Renata Condi. -- 2. ed. -- São Paulo : Moderna, 2019. -- (Students for peace)

Obra em 4 v. do 6º ao 9º ano.

1. Inglês (Ensino fundamental) I. Condi, Renata. II. Título. III. Série.

19-26387 CDD-372.652

Índices para catálogo sistemático:
1. Inglês : Ensino fundamental 372.652
Maria Paula C. Riyuzo - Bibliotecária - CRB-8/7639

ISBN 978-85-16-12048-1 (LA)
ISBN 978-85-16-12049-8 (LP)

Reprodução proibida. Art. 184 do Código Penal e Lei 9.610 de 19 de fevereiro de 1998.

Todos os direitos reservados.

Richmond
Editora Moderna Ltda.
Rua Padre Adelino, 758 - Belenzinho
São Paulo - SP - Brasil - CEP 03303-904
www.richmond.com.br
2019

Impresso no Brasil

Créditos das fotos: Capa: RadomanDurkovic/Istockphoto; p. 6: MoustacheGirl/IstockphotoMoustacheGirl/Istockphoto; p. 8: Dragon Images/Istockphoto; Fernando Bueno/Pulsar Imagens; Desifoto/Istockphoto; p. 9: Maica/Istockphoto; Damedeeso/Istockphoto; MicroStockHub/Istockphoto; MicroStockHub/Istockphoto; NoraVector/Istockphoto; p. 12: Rafael Olechoski/Istockphoto; p. 13: Traveler 1116/Istockphoto; digitalreflections/Shutterstock; p. 14: Acervo pessoal; Usborne Publishing; mastertronic; Ben Harding/Istockphoto; p. 16: Reprodução; Reprodução; Reprodução; p. 17: Whitewish/Istockphoto; Vitorcvetkovic/Istockphoto; Alleko/Istockphoto; Poligrafistka/Istockphoto; p. 18: Reprodução; p. 20: franckreporter/Istockphoto; p. 21: DragonImages/Istockphoto; Steve Debenport/Istockphoto; vadimguzhva/Istockphoto; p. 22: Your Community Blog; p. 23: IMDB; p. 25: ULU_BIRD/Istockphoto; BahadirTanriover/Istockphoto; Pollyana Ventura/Istockphoto; llvllagic/Istockphoto; trekandshoot/Istockphoto; PeskyMonkey/Istockphoto; Petar Mulaj/Istockphoto; WoodyAlec/Istockphoto; André Muller/Istockphoto; Sisoje/Istockphoto; p. 26: rolandtopor/Istockphoto; p. 27: carlos cardetas/Alamy/Fotoarena; Universal Pictures/Illumination Entertainment/Alamy/Fotoarena; p. 29: Sydney Nalinkarn; browndogstudios/Istockphoto; furtaev/Istockphoto; Tanya St/Istockphoto; milkghost/Istockphoto; Gunay Aliyeva/Istockphoto; Alex Belomlinsky/Istockphoto; bubaone/Istockphoto; bubaone/Istockphoto; Lara2017/Istockphoto; Makkuro_GL/Istockphoto; p. 32: PeopleImages/Istockphoto; p. 33: ©United Nations, Art for Peace Contest, submitted by Prinsa S. Kathmandu, Nepal; p. 34: CBS Photo/Getty Images; p. 35: Universal Pictures/courtesy Everett Collection/Fotoarena; Romulo Fialdini/Tempo Composto/Tarsila do Amaral Empreendimentos; Acervo Museu Lasar Segall - IBRAN/MinC; p. 36: ©2010 Signe Wilkinson / Dist. by Andrews McMeel Syndication for UFS; p. 37: Jerry Craft; ©2017 Todd Clark / Dist. by Andrews McMeel Syndication; p. 38: ©2017 Todd Clark / Dist. by Andrews McMeel Syndication; p. 39: Richard Cartwright/CBS Photo Archive via Getty Images; Robert Voets/CBS Photo Archive/Getty Images; Robert Voets/CBS Photo Archive/Getty Images; CBS Photo Archive/Getty Images; Justin Lubin/CBS Photo Archive/Getty Images; CBS Photo Archive/Getty Images; p. 40: Jerry Craft; p. 41: ©2010 Signe Wilkinson / Dist. by Andrews McMeel Syndication for UFS; Jerry Craft; p. 42: Warner Bros. Entertainment Inc. All Rights Reserved; p. 43: monkeybusinessimages/Istockphoto; p. 44: Earl Gibson III/AFP; p. 46: PLUNKETT/Reuters/Latinstock; Fabio Colombini; ANDRES STAPF/Reuters/Latinstock; p. 47: CAREN FIROUZ/Reuters/Latinstock; p. 48: Bodnar Taras/Shutterstock; p. 52: ngirish/Istockphoto; Stock2You/Shutterstock; p. 53: andresr/Istockphoto; p. 54: Antonio_Diaz/Istockphoto; subjug/Istockphoto; p. 56: Life of Mummy; p. 58: Youth Change; The Silver Lining Foundation; p. 59: Andrew Wales; p. 60: mixetto/Istockphoto; kate_sept2004/Istockphoto; Rawpixel/Shutterstock; p. 61: Highwaystarz-Photography/Istockphoto; monkeybusinessimages/Istockphoto; Andrey_Popov/Shutterstock; p. 63: RichVintage/Istockphoto; RapidEye/Istockphoto; Nasjonalgalleriet, Oslo, Norway; Lolostock/Shutterstock; Malombra76/Istockphoto; SensorSpot/Istockphoto; p. 65: adamkaz/Istockphoto; Ben-Schonewille/Istockphoto; burakkarademir/Istockphoto; Deagreez/Istockphoto; Syda Productions/Shutterstock; MartinPrescott/Istockphoto; Solovyova/Istockphoto; Milles Studio/Shutterstock; p. 66: filistimlyanin/Istockphoto; p. 67: Stígur Már Karlsson/Heimsmyndir/Istockphoto; p. 68: manonallard/Istockphoto; SerrNovik/Istockphoto; g-stockstudio/Istockphoto; FatCamera/Istockphoto; p. 72: tomass2015/Istockphoto; p. 73: Tim Rooke/Shutterstock; Jose CABEZAS/AFP; p. 75: MarVista Entertainment; p. 76: hocus-focus/Istockphoto; milanvirijevic/Istockphoto; marchmeena29/Istockphoto; Rawf8/Istockphoto; p. 77: NeonShot/Istockphoto; Dirtydog_Creative/Istockphoto; Farknot_Architect/Istockphoto; nicomenijes/Istockphoto; Reprodução; Reprodução; p. 79: MarVista Entertainment; courtneyk/Istockphoto; p. 80: Chris Brunskill Ltd/Getty Images; ayzek/Istockphoto; Vanessa Carvalho/Brazil Photo Press/AFP; ayzek/Istockphoto; Monica Schipper/FilmMagic/Getty Images; ayzek/Istockphoto; Jim Spellman/WireImage/Getty Images; ayzek/Istockphoto; Frazer Harrison/LARAS/AFP; ayzek/Istockphoto; PIUS UTOMI EKPEI/AFP; ayzek/Istockphoto; Daniel Bockwoldt/Getty Images; ayzek/Istockphoto; Juan Naharro Gimenez/WireImage/Getty Images; ayzek/Istockphoto; p. 81: MarVista Entertainment; p. 82: Steve Debenport/Istockphoto; p. 84: woraput/Istockphoto; p. 86: garymilner/Istockphoto; Age Fotostock/Easypix Brasil; Artfoliophoto/Istockphoto; p. 87: Widhibek/Shuttestock; FatCamera/Istockphoto; nevereverro/Istockphoto; p. 88: Hiranandani Hospital; p. 89: sportsplex; p. 91: bubaone/Istockphoto; p. 92: 1MoreCreative/Istockphoto; JBryson/Istockphoto; CHEN WS/Shutterstock; leolintang/Istockphoto; imtmphoto/Istockphoto; Joseph Calomeni/Istockphoto; p. 93: andresr/Istockphoto; p. 94: Mikkaphoto/Istockphoto; p. 95: Daegu International School; p. 98: pixdeluxe/Istockphoto; Mike Ray/Barcroft USA/Getty Images; Constantinis/Istockphoto; p. 99: scyther5/Istockphoto; SolStock/Istockphoto; fstop123/Istockphoto; damircudic/Istockphoto; eli_asenova/Istockphoto; p. 100: The Journey Through Autism; p. 101: El and Jae; p. 103: ©1980 Paws, Inc. All Rights Reserved / Dist. by Andrews McMeel Syndication; ©1982 Paws, Inc. All Rights Reserved / Dist. by Andrews McMeel Syndication; ©2005 Paws, Inc. All Rights Reserved / Dist. by Andrews McMeel Syndication; p. 104: ©2016 Paws, Inc. All Rights Reserved / Dist. by Andrews McMeel Syndication; ©1980 Paws, Inc. All Rights Reserved / Dist. by Andrews McMeel Syndication; p. 105: calvindexter/Istockphoto; calvindexter/Istockphoto; calvindexter/Istockphoto; calvindexter/Istockphoto; p. 106: -VICTOR-/Istockphoto; appleuzr/Istockphoto; leremy/Istockphoto; appleuzr/Istockphoto; appleuzr/Istockphoto; igorshi/Istockphoto; appleuzr/Istockphoto; appleuzr/Istockphoto; appleuzr/Istockphoto; gigavector/Istockphoto; appleuzr/Istockphoto; AVIcons/Istockphoto; p. 107: Vox Pops International; wdstock/Istockphoto; p. 110: Melanie Stetson Freeman/The Christian Science Monitor/Getty Images; Robert Cianflone/Getty Images; Jakkrit Orrasri/Shutterstock; CHRISTOPHE SIMON/AFP/GettyImages; p. 114: acavalli/Istockphoto; Nikada/Istockphoto; Sidekick/Istockphoto; Dean Mitchell/Istockphoto; monkeybusinessimages/Istockphoto; katkov/Istockphoto; skynesher/Istockphoto; p. 115: monkeybusinessimages/Istockphoto; 541292444/Istockphoto; GreenPimp/Istockphoto; Buda Mendes/Getty Images; Spotmatik/Istockphoto; Angela Weiss/Getty Images; Clive Rose/Getty Images; p. 116: monkeybusinessimages/Istockphoto; malerapaso/Istockphoto; man_kukuku/Istockphoto; Kikovic/Istockphoto; p. 117: Dean Mitchell/Istockphoto; Eva-Katalin/Istockphoto; digitalskillet/Istockphoto; FG Trade/Istockphoto; FG Trade/Istockphoto; Ridofranz/Istockphoto; PeopleImages/Istockphoto; Damir Khabirov/Istockphoto; darrya/Istockphoto; ajr_images/Istockphoto; FG Trade/Istockphoto; kate_sept2004/Istockphoto; Igor Alecsander/Istockphoto; uschools/Istockphoto; Steve Debenport/Istockphoto; JohnnyGreig/Istockphoto; romrodinka/Istockphoto; Travel Stock/Shutterstock; Omer Messinger/ZUMA Wire/Fotoarena; p. 120: baibaz/Istockphoto; fstop123/Istockphoto; Wavebreakmedia/Istockphoto; Imgorthand/Istockphoto; Milkos/Istockphoto; PeopleImages/Istockphoto; p. 121: django/Istockphoto; p. 124: grimgram/Istockphoto; Wavebreakmedia/Istockphoto; Squaredpixels/Istockphoto; EvgeniyShkolenko/Istockphoto; Denis Makarenko/Shutterstock; JC Olivera/Getty Images; Giuseppe Maffia/NurPhoto via Getty Images; Melanie Lemahieu/Shutterstock; p. 125: oatawa/Istockphoto; p. 126: luminis/Istockphoto; Suradech Prapairat/Shutterstock; Eshma/Istockphoto; venakr/Istockphoto; KoKimk/Istockphoto; popovaphoto/Istockphoto; ImageDB/Istockphoto; All-stock-photos/Shutterstock; p. 127: Zinyange Auntony/AFP; p. 128: mediaphotos/Istockphoto; technotr/Istockphoto; skynesher/Istockphoto; Tashi-Delek/Istockphoto; p. 142: Fox Film; Dragonfly Books; p. 143: Columbia Pictures; Quirk Books; Amulet Books.

CÓPIA NÃO AUTORIZADA É CRIME
ABDR
ASSOCIAÇÃO BRASILEIRA DE DIREITOS REPROGRÁFICOS
RESPEITE O DIREITO AUTORAL

Dear student,

This is **Students for PEACE** – a set of materials designed not only to help you learn English, but also to make you think about, discuss and act upon important issues related to your life and your community. **Students for PEACE** is the result of many years of study and research.

When we first sat down to write this series, we felt that we had to go beyond the study of the English language because there was something the world needed desperately – peace. And it still needs it. So we decided to make peace education the core of this series and its goal. The ideas presented in **Students for PEACE** are based on the positive concept of peace as justice, tolerance and respect.

This series will certainly help you learn English, but we hope they will also help you understand and acknowledge human diversity and live with one another in harmony, facing the different challenges of the world around you.

As those famous song lyrics said, "All we are saying is give peace a chance!"

Have a nice year!

Editorial team

Scope & sequence

Welcome Chapter (p. 6) — Let's get to know your book!

	Goals	Explore & Studio	Building blocks & Toolbox	Sync – Listening & Sync – Speaking
1 **English everywhere** (p. 8)	• Explore dialogues from a spelling bee competition. • Identify the presence of words in English in our daily life. • Read and write bilingual dictionary entries. • Recognize similarities and differences in the pronunciation of some English and Brazilian Portuguese words. • Role-play a spelling bee competition. • Understand the process of cultural integration. • Understand the use of the genitive case ('s).	• Dictionary entry	• English and Brazilian Portuguese words • Genitive case ('s)	• Spelling Bee • At the Spelling Bee
2 **Identities** (p. 20)	• Identify cognates in a text as a way to understand a second language. • Reflect on what factors make up our identity. • Understand and create a self-introduction. • Understand and write photo captions. • Understand the use of numbers from 1 to 101. • Understand the use of the verb "to be" to talk and write about ourselves and other people.	• Photo caption • Scrapbook	• Numbers • Verb "to be"	• This is me • My presentation
Peace talk (p. 32)	We all are one			
3 **Family** (p. 34)	• Interview someone in order to make an oral presentation. • Learn vocabulary for family members. • Listen to people talk about family relationships. • Read and create comic strips about families. • Review the genitive case ('s) to describe family relationships. • Understand and create a family tree. • Understand the use of possessive adjectives and pronouns.	• Comic strip	• Family members • Possessive adjectives/ Review the genitive case ('s)	• Interview • Interview about your family
4 **School life** (p. 46)	• Compare different types of schools all over the world. • Identify the days of the week, time and school subjects. • Read and create a paragraph describing your school timetable. • Read and create a school timetable. • Talk about your study routine. • Understand someone talking about homeschooling. • Use "at", "in", "on", "from… to" with adverbs of time. • Use the present simple affirmative to describe daily school routines.	• Timetable	• Exploring a school timetable: vocabulary and time • Present simple: affirmative	• Homeschooling • Talking about your study routine
Peace talk (p. 58)	Be a buddy, not a bully			

	Goals	Explore & Studio	Building blocks & Toolbox	Sync – Listening & Sync – Speaking
5 **Connected** (p. 60)	• Talk about your chores at home, at school and/ or in your neighborhood. • Understand a teenager talking about her household chores. • Understand and create memes. • Understand the different uses of the affirmative, negative and interrogative forms of the present simple. • Understand the use of adverbs of frequency. • Understand the use of verbs related to household chores.	• Meme	• Household chores verbs/ Adverbs of frequency • Present simple (affirmative, negative, interrogative)	• My household chores • Talking about my chores
6 **Networking** (p. 72)	• Learn the adjectives for some nationalities. • Learn the names of some countries and the continents. • Simulate spoken dialogues (greeting people, introducing yourself and asking what the other person is doing). • Understand a dialogue between two teenagers who have just met. • Understand and use the present continuous. • Understand and write text messages.	• Text message	• Countries, nationalities and continents • Present continuous	• Meeting a new friend • Greeting someone
Peace talk (p. 84)	Building social skills			
7 **Sports** (p. 86)	• Learn the names of body parts. • Learn the use of the imperative. • Reflect on the importance of practicing sports in order to maintain a healthy lifestyle. • Understand and create a poster about sports and health. • Understand and do a survey on sports and health. • Understand and use words related to sports. • Use the imperative to make recommendations.	• Poster	• Sports and parts of the body • Imperative	• Asking and answering questions about sports • A survey on sports
8 **This is me** (p. 98)	• Deliver a presentation about your free-time activities. • Learn how to use verb patterns with "hate", "like" and "love" + "to". • Raise awareness of the importance of leisure time in our lives. • Review the use of the present continuous. • Review the use of the present simple. • Understand and write texts for the "About me" section of blogs. • Understand different people talking about their leisure activities.	• "About me" blog section	• Free-time activities • Present simple and present continuous (review), verb pattern ("hate", "like", "love" + "to")	• What do you do in your free time? • Presentation about free-time activities
Peace talk (p. 110)	Sportsmanship			

Self-assessment 112
Workbook 113
Language reference 129
Interdisciplinary project 134
Transcripts 136
Glossary 139
Learning more 142
Track list 144
References 144

Welcome to Students for PEACE!
Let's get to know your book!

1 Explore the book and answer the questions, using the map as a guide. Follow your teacher's instructions.

a Na página 14, há a capa de um livro de literatura inglesa sobre uma menina chamada Alice. Quem é o seu autor?

_____

b Na página 29, conheceremos uma estudante intercambista da Tailândia. Qual é o nome dela?

_____

c O Capítulo 3 apresenta uma família de uma série de televisão estadunidense. Qual é o nome dessa série?

_____

d Vá até o Capítulo 4. Em que país está localizada a escola Mashal Model School?

_____

e Localize os memes do Capítulo 5. Que quadro famoso com a imagem de uma mulher foi usado como inspiração para um dos memes? Esse quadro, pintado por Leonardo da Vinci, é mundialmente conhecido e está em exibição no museu do Louvre, em Paris.

_____

f Na página 81, há uma atividade sobre uma adolescente que se mudou para outro país. Para qual país ela se mudou?

_____

g O Capítulo 7 é sobre esportes. Na página 89, há um cartaz que menciona três esportes. Quais são eles?

_____

h No Capítulo 8, há um gato famoso. Qual é o nome dele?

_____

2 **Let's get to know the book. Answer the questions.**

a Quantos capítulos há no livro? Quais seções compõem cada um?

_____

b Que outras seções há depois do último capítulo, logo após o componente "Peace talk – Chapters 7 and 8"?

_____

c Dos assuntos abordados nos capítulos, há algum que lhe instigou mais a curiosidade? Se sim, qual e por quê? Compartilhe com um/a colega.

1 English everywhere

Goals

- Explore dialogues from a spelling bee competition.
- Identify the presence of words in English in our daily life.
- Read and write bilingual dictionary entries.
- Recognize similarities and differences in the pronunciation of some English and Brazilian Portuguese words.
- Role-play a spelling bee competition.
- Understand the process of cultural integration.
- Understand the use of the genitive case ('s).

Spark

1 Talk to your classmates about these questions.

a Which word is not related to any of the pictures above? Circle it.

> dictionary   dog   hamburger   pizza   remote control   social media   subway

b What words in English do you see in the pictures? Write them.

_____

_____

_____

8

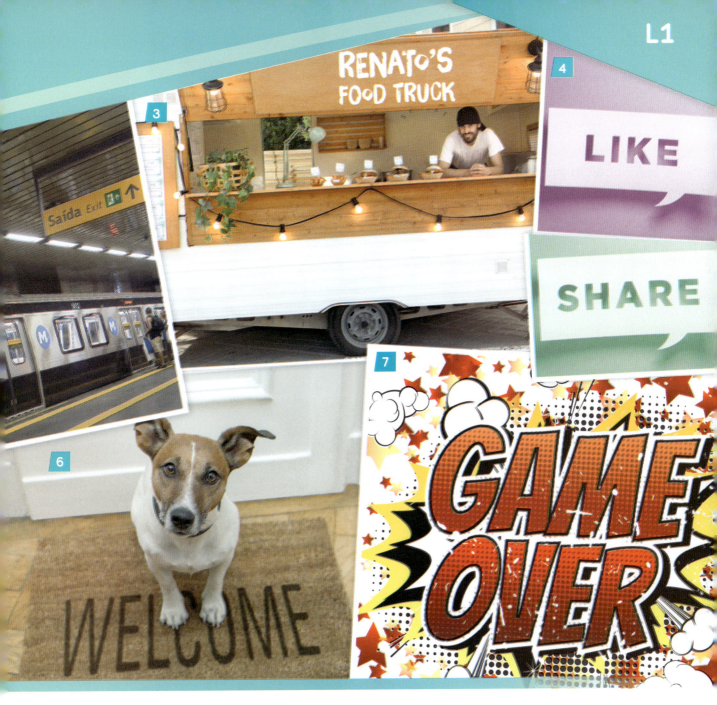

c Do you see words in English around your school or on your way home? Make a list.

Going further

Look around your classroom. Can you find anything written in English? Share your findings with your classmates.

L1

Explore Dictionary entry

Pre-reading

1 Look at the texts in activity 2. Then check the appropriate options.

- a ☐ These types of texts are normally found in magazines.
- b ☐ These types of texts are usually found in dictionaries.
- c ☐ Text 1 is a type of text normally found on the internet.
- d ☐ Text 2 is a type of online text written collaboratively by volunteers.
- e ☐ Both texts contain English words translated into Portuguese.
- f ☐ The target audience of these types of texts are people interested in learning Portuguese.
- g ☐ The objective of these types of texts is to inform.

> **Language clue**
> **entry** = a word listed in a dictionary

Reading

2 Read texts 1 and 2 and check.

a Which text helped you understand the meaning of the word "welcome"?

☐ Text 1.   ☐ Text 2.

b Why?

☐ Clear examples.   ☐ Quantity of information.
☐ Organization of the text.   Other: _____

Text 1

welcher s. o m.q. *welsher*

Welchman s. o m.q. *Welshman*

welcome s. boas-vindas, boa acolhida; recepção cordial. **-to bid someone w.** dar as boas-vindas a alguém. **-to give warm w.** demonstrar muita alegria na chegada de alguém; resistir vigorosamente. [...] / a. bem-vindo, bem recebido (*a welcome guest*), grato, agradável, aceitável. **-to be w. to** ter toda a liberdade de, estar à vontade para (*you are welcome to do it* você tem toda a liberdade de fazê-lo); [...] **-to make someone w.** dar bom acolhimento a alguém. **-you are w.** de nada, não há de quê (resposta a um agradecimento) / *interj*. bem-vindo!, salve! / *vt.* dar as boas-vindas; receber, saudar (quem chega); acolher com prazer, com alegria

welcomely *adv*. hospitaleiramente, com prazer, com alegria; agradavelmente; em boa hora

weld s. solda, soldadura, caldeamento; junta (de solda); (bot.) lírio-dos-tintureiros, tinta dessa planta / *vt.* soldar; caldear; (fig.) unir, fundir, consolidar / *vi.* soldar-se, caldear-se

HOUAISS, A. (Ed.). ***Webster's Dicionário Inglês-Português***. Atualizado. Rio de Janeiro: Record, 1998. p. 874.

Text 2

welcome

Índice [mostrar]

Inglês [editar]

Adjetivo [editar]
welcome
1. bem-vindo

Interjeição [editar]
welcome
1. bem-vindo

Substantivo [editar]
welcome
1. recepção
2. boas-vindas

Expressões [editar]
- you're welcome:

Verbo [editar]
welcome
1. receber, acolher

Etimologia [editar]
Do inglês médio *welcome*, *wolcume*, *wulcume*, *wilcume*, do inglês antigo *wilcuma* e do proto-germânico *wiljakwumô*.

Pronúncia [editar]
- **AFI:** /ˈwɛl.kəm/

Categorias: Entrada com etimologia (Inglês) | Entrada com pronúncia (Inglês) | Adjetivo (Inglês) | Interjeição (Inglês) | Substantivo (Inglês) | Verbo (Inglês)

Adapted from <https://pt.wiktionary.org/wiki/welcome>. Accessed on February 22, 2019.

3 Read texts 1 and 2 again. Then check the appropriate option for each item.

a According to text 2, which word classes can the word "welcome" belong to?
- ☐ Adjective, conjunction, noun and verb.
- ☐ Adjective, interjection, noun and verb.
- ☐ Adjective, interjection, pronoun and verb.

b Text 1 also mentions the word classes for the word "welcome". What are they?
- ☐ Noun, adjective, interjection and transitive verb.
- ☐ Noun, adverb, interjection and intransitive verb.
- ☐ Noun, adverb, interjection and transitive verb.

L1

4 **Check the appropriate options.**

a In text 1, the expressions with "welcome" are presented...
- [ ] in bold and preceded by a hyphen (-).
- [ ] after the initials "vt".

b The solution used to make text 1 shorter is...
- [ ] the use of a hyphen before the words in bold.
- [ ] the use of "w." to avoid repeating the word "welcome".

c The meaning of the expression "You are welcome" is in...
- [ ] text 1.
- [ ] text 2.
- [ ] both texts.

Post-reading

5 **Discuss these questions with your classmates.**

a Why do users choose one type of dictionary rather than the other one? Check the possible reason(s).
- [ ] They can explore the hyperlinks.
- [ ] They can hear the pronunciation.
- [ ] They believe paper dictionaries have more credibility.

b Check other types of dictionaries that you know. Tell your classmates about them.
- [ ] Monolingual
- [ ] Encyclopedia
- [ ] Thesaurus

c Text 2 represents an online collaborative dictionary. What are some of the pros and cons of using this type of dictionary? Write *P* (pros) or *C* (cons).
- [ ] The information may be incorrect.
- [ ] The meanings may be constantly updated.
- [ ] People can correct the information if there is something wrong about it.
- [ ] The meanings of the words may be contradictory.
- [ ] People from different backgrounds can contribute with information.
- [ ] People may distort information.

Language clue

pros and cons = advantages and disadvantages

Going further

Wiktionary is a combination of "wiki" and "dictionary". The word "wiki" means "very quick" in Hawaiian.

Toolbox Genitive case ('s)

1 Look at the pictures and circle the options that make the sentences true.

a The person in picture 1 is the **inspirer/author/translator** of the dictionary in picture 2.

b The person in picture 1 is **a contemporary/an old/an unknown** lexicographer.

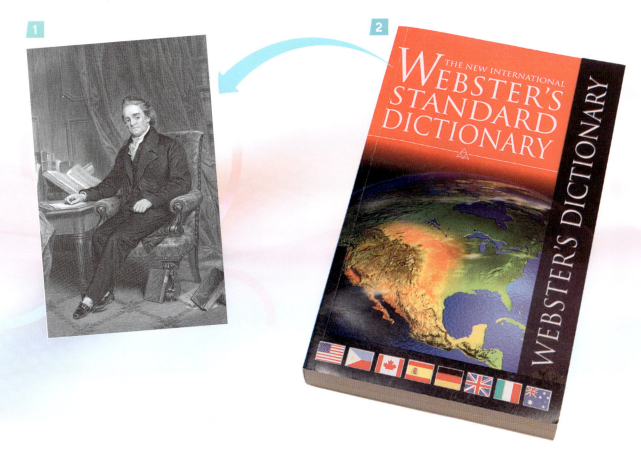

> **Going further**
> The word "Webster" is linked to Noah Webster (1758-1843), the creator of *An American Dictionary of the English Language* (1828), the first American dictionary to present word definitions with clear and complete explanations.

2 Look at the dictionary cover in activity 1. Check the appropriate option.

a The apostrophe + s ('s) after the word "Webster" is used to…

☐ indicate plural.

☐ indicate who possesses or who is associated with this word.

b To indicate that something belongs to somebody, we use…

☐ the name of the person + 's + the thing possessed.

☐ the thing possessed + 's + the name of the person.

L2

3 Study the four examples. Then complete the sentences using the words from the box.

> Alice   Shakespeare   teachers   Wallace and Gromit

a The places mentioned in the title of this folder belong or are related to _____.

b The character who has the adventures mentioned in the title of this book is _____.

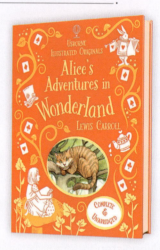

c The characters who have the adventures mentioned in the title of this game are _____.

d The sign shows that this room is reserved for the _____.

4 Read the sentences. Then underline the appropriate options.

a In *Wallace and Gromit's Grand Adventures*, the *'s* means that Wallace and Gromit have **the same/different** adventures.

b In "Teachers' room", the *'* means that this is a room for **only one teacher/many teachers**.

c We use **'s/'** after two or more nouns when the thing or action is linked to all of them.

d We use **'s/'** after plural nouns, like "teachers", "students", "girls" and "boys".

Building blocks: English and Brazilian Portuguese words

1 Observe the words and do the activities.

I bike	IV e-mail	VII jeans	X skate
II delivery	V enter	VIII rap	XI surf
III DJ	VI hot dog	IX shampoo	XII video game

a These are words in English that are also used in Brazil. Classify them in the chart.

Clothes/Cosmetics	Computer-related words	Food	Sports/Music/Entertainment	Types of service

b How do you pronounce each of these words?

2 🎧 2 Listen and repeat the words. Do you say them the same way when you use these English words in Brazilian contexts?

3 Discuss the questions with your classmates.

a Do you listen to songs or watch movies in English? Are there any words and expressions you learned from a song or a movie?

b What is your opinion about the influence of English-speaking countries in the songs and movies we watch in Brazil?
☐ I think it is OK.   ☐ I don't think it is OK.

c What do you think about the influence that the culture from those countries have on our culture?
☐ I think it is OK.   ☐ I think it is inevitable.   ☐ I don't like it.

4 🎧 3 Listen to foreigners saying some Brazilian Portuguese words. Check the word they do not say.

☐ açaí   ☐ feijoada   ☐ mosquito
☐ capoeira   ☐ guaraná   ☐ samba
☐ farofa   ☐ lambada   ☐ tapioca

5 Do you think the words in activity 4 are pronounced in the same way by English-speaking people and by Brazilians?

6 Check the possible answers.
Words in English are used in Brazilian contexts because…

a ☐ Brazil was a British colony.   c ☐ most social networking services are from the United States.
b ☐ technology often comes from English-speaking countries.

7 Go back to activity 1. What other English words and expressions are frequently used in Brazil? Make a list on your notebook and share it with your classmates.

L3

Sync Listening: **Spelling Bee**

Pre-listening

1 Look at the pictures and talk to a partner about them.

a What type of program is it?

☐ A talk show.   ☐ A competition.   ☐ A cartoon.

b What do people do in this type of TV program? Check all possible options.

☐ They compete against other people.   ☐ They talk about their schools.
☐ They spell words.   ☐ They test their history skills.

c Would it be nice to participate in a program like this?

Listening

2 🎧 4 Listen to a part of the *Spelling Bee* TV show. Check the appropriate options.

> **Language clue**
> **contestant** = competitor, player, participant

a To take part in the competition, we need…

☐ to spell the word twice.   ☐ to say the word and spell it.   ☐ to have a dictionary.

b The pieces of information mentioned about the contestant are…

☐ his first name and last name.   ☐ his name and age.   ☐ the school where he goes to and his age.

3 🎧 4 Listen to the extract again and check the appropriate options.

a The participant spells the word in the following way:

☐ A-C-C-O-M-O-D-A-T-E.   ☐ A-C-O-M-O-D-A-T-E.
☐ A-C-C-O-M M-O-D-A-T-E.

b The pronouncer tells the participant that the correct spelling of the word is…

☐ A-C-C-O-M-O-D-A-T-E.   ☐ A-C-O-M-O-D-A-T-E.
☐ A-C-C-O-M-M-O-D-A-T-E.

4 🎧 5 How do you say the letters of the alphabet in English? Listen and repeat.

A B C D E F G H I J K L M N O P Q R S T U V W X Y Z

> **Useful language**
> How do you spell...?

5 🎧 6 Listen to another part of the *Spelling Bee*. Write the words from the box in the appropriate spaces.

burrito   Jonathan   sevruga   Victoria

a Name of contestant: _____

Word: _____

b Name of contestant: _____

Word: _____

Post-listening

6 Answer and share.

a The contestants spell words that are not of English origin. Use them to complete the sentences.

_____ is of Spanish origin.   _____ is of Russian origin.

b Think of food-related words of foreign origin used in Brazil. Make a list.

_____

7 Work in groups. Play "Tic-Tac-Toe".

L3

Sync Speaking: At the Spelling Bee

Pre-speaking

1 What pieces of information about a spelling bee contestant are usually mentioned? Check all possible options.

- ⬤ first name and last name
- ⬤ school where he/she studies
- ⬤ favorite movie
- ⬤ city where he/she lives
- ⬤ age
- ⬤ plans for the future

2 Read the beginning of a contestant's presentation. What pieces of information from activity 1 do the presenters mention?

> Our first contestant is Victoria Smolen. She is twelve years old, from Onondaga Hill Middle School. All right, Victoria! The first word this afternoon is...

Extract from the audio available at <https://www.youtube.com/watch?v=9QAWJdItVkk>. Accessed on February 11, 2019.

3 Use the model in activity 2 to write your own presentation.

_____

_____

Speaking

4 Now, in groups, role-play a spelling bee.

Useful language

Numbers
- 10 ten
- 11 eleven
- 12 twelve
- 13 thirteen
- 14 fourteen
- 15 fifteen
- 16 sixteen
- 17 seventeen
- 18 eighteen
- 19 nineteen

Useful language

That's correct!
Well done!
Sorry... Try again.
Almost there!

Post-speaking

5 What was easy and difficult for you in this production? Write *E* (easy) or *D* (difficult).

- ☐ Spell the words.
- ☐ Be a contestant.
- ☐ Remember the letters of the alphabet.
- ☐ Be a presenter.

 **Studio** Dictionary entry

> **What:** a dictionary entry
> **To whom:** for personal use; other students
> **Media:** paper; digital
> **Objective:** organize new words

1. Make a list of the new words in this chapter.
2. Find the words in a bilingual dictionary. Write their meanings.
3. Write or draw examples.
4. Share your work with a partner.
5. Give feedback to your partner.
6. Revise your text.
7. Organize the words in alphabetical order.
8. Share your work with your classmates.
9. Put all the words together and make a class **dictionary**!
10. Publish your work on the **Students for PEACE Social Media** <www.studentsforpeace.com.br>, using the tag **dictionaryentry** or others chosen by the students.

2 Identities

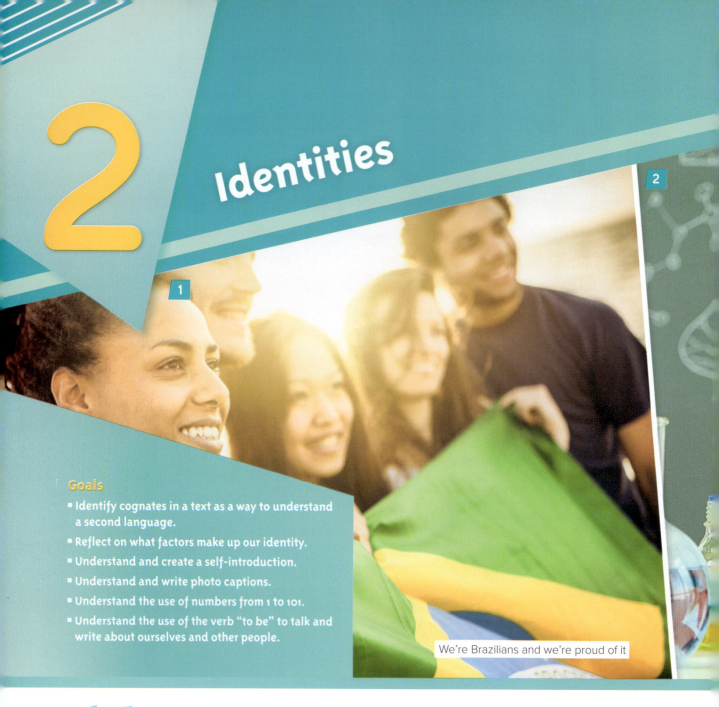

Goals
- Identify cognates in a text as a way to understand a second language.
- Reflect on what factors make up our identity.
- Understand and create a self-introduction.
- Understand and write photo captions.
- Understand the use of numbers from 1 to 101.
- Understand the use of the verb "to be" to talk and write about ourselves and other people.

We're Brazilians and we're proud of it

Spark

1 Talk to your classmates about these questions.

a Look at the pictures. What do you see? Number the descriptions accordingly.

☐ A group of friends with a flag.
☐ A father and his son playing video game.
☐ A student in the science lab.
☐ A goalkeeper in a soccer match.

b Different factors make up our identity. What factors do you see in the pictures? Check.

☐ age
☐ appearance
☐ interests
☐ origin

Other: _____

Our goalkeeper rocks

My best student

My son

c Suppose you are going to meet someone for the first time. What would you like to know about this person? Check.

- [ ] age
- [ ] best friend's name
- [ ] family
- [ ] favorite team
- [ ] name
- [ ] nationality
- [ ] school

Other: _____

Going further

In our society, there are many situations in which we have to show documents to prove our identity, such as birth certificate, identity card, passport, driver's license, student card etc. Which one(s) do you have?

L1

Explore Photo caption

Pre-reading

1 Look at the pictures in texts 1 and 2 and read the descriptions below. Write the numbers of the corresponding texts.

☐ Will Smith and Jaden Smith. ☐ A scene from a movie.
☐ A woman and a child. ☐ Two actors posing for a photographer.

Text 1

Available at <http://www.cbc.ca/newsblogs/yourcommunity/2013/05/will-smiths-anti-girlfriend-advice-great-says-teen-son.html>.
Accessed on February 14, 2019.

Going further

Photo captions provide the reader with useful information about the picture. They may contain names of people, things and places, as well as dates and descriptions. It is common to use the present tense of verbs in captions. It is important to indicate the position of people in the picture to help readers identify who is who, as in this example:

Text 2

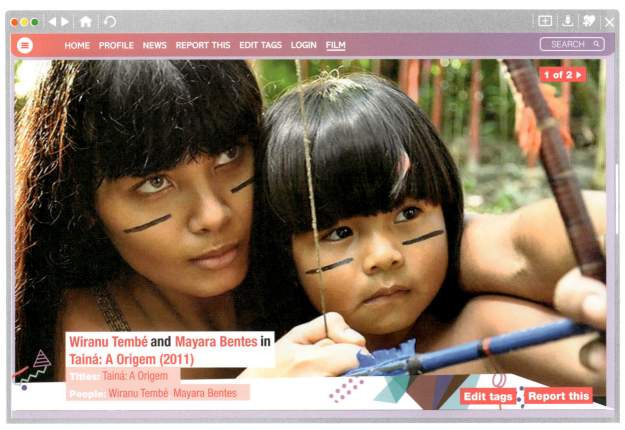

Available at <http://www.imdb.com/title/tt1708510/mediaviewer/rm310851328>. Accessed on February 14, 2019.

2 Check the appropriate options about the pictures in activity 1.

a I can see these kinds of pictures in...
- [ ] newspapers, magazines and blogs.
- [ ] documents that show someone's identity.

b They are used to...
- [ ] grab the reader's attention.
- [ ] fill in blank spaces on a page.
- [ ] help tell a piece of news or a fact to the reader.

3 Now look at the photo captions in activity 1. Check the items that are true.
Captions...

a [ ] help contextualize the photo.
b [ ] add technical details about the photo.
c [ ] give important information about the photo.
d [ ] identify the people or the fact depicted in the photo.
e [ ] explain where people are in a photo (right, left, between, next to).
f [ ] criticize the people who appear in the photo.

> **Useful language**
>
> When you don't know the meaning of a word in English, you can ask "What does (word) mean?" or "What's the meaning of (word)?"

L1

Reading

4 Read the texts in activity 1 and check the appropriate columns.

	Text 1	Text 2
a It is from a blog.		
b It is from a photo gallery.		
c It has a photo with a caption.		
d It has a caption with just one sentence.		
e It has a caption with hyperlinks.		
f It has a caption with a photo credit.		
g It has a caption including people's first name and surname.		
h It has a caption identifying people's position in the photo.		

5 Complete the chart with information from the texts, whenever possible. Put an "X" to indicate pieces of information not available in the texts.

	Text 1	Text 2
Names (actors and actresses)		
Title of the movie		
Year of the movie		
Credits (photo)		

6 Find cognates in text 1 for the following items.

a Two of the blog categories: _____

b Will Smith's nationality: _____

c Will Smith's profession: _____

d Type of event Will and Jaden Smith participated in: _____

> **Language clue**
>
> **cognate** = a word in a language with the same origin as a word in another language (e.g.: event/ *evento*; profession/*profissão* etc.)

RTV

Watch:
Similar words

Post-reading

7 Discuss these questions with your classmates.

a When you see photos in a text, do you usually read the captions?

b Suppose the photos in texts 1 and 2 had no captions. Would you understand the two contexts?

Building blocks Numbers

1 Look at the pictures. They all show numbers in digits. Match them to the numbers in their word form.

- [ ] one
- [ ] two
- [ ] three
- [ ] four
- [ ] five
- [ ] six
- [ ] seven
- [ ] eight
- [ ] nine
- [ ] ten

L2

2 🎧 7 Add the missing letters to the numerals in their word form. Then listen, check and repeat.

11	eleven	25	twenty-☐☐☐☐
12	twelve	26	twenty-☐☐☐
13	thirteen	27	twenty-☐☐☐☐☐
14	☐☐☐☐teen	28	twenty-☐☐☐☐☐
15	fifteen	29	twenty-☐☐☐☐
16	☐☐☐teen	30	thirty
17	☐☐☐☐☐teen	40	forty
18	☐☐☐☐☐een	50	fifty
19	☐☐☐☐teen	60	☐☐☐ty
20	twenty	70	☐☐☐☐☐ty
21	twenty-one	80	☐☐☐☐☐y
22	twenty-☐☐☐	90	☐☐☐☐ty
23	twenty-☐☐☐☐☐	100	one hundred
24	twenty-☐☐☐☐	101	one hundred (and)☐☐☐

3 Play the "Apple Tree" game. Follow the instructions.

a Choose a number. Then draw a line for each letter in this number (e.g.: for "one", draw three lines).

b Have your classmates guess the number by saying alphabet letters.

c Cross out the apples as the guesses are used up. Good luck!

Toolbox Verb "to be"

1 Read these extracts from a book called *Kids Speak: Children Talk about Themselves*. Then check the appropriate option.

Text 1

SHORTY

My name is Ze'ev. I'm in fifth grade. I'm not really special in any way — not in schoolwork or in sports, and not socially either.

WALDER, Chaim. *Kids Speak:* Children Talk about Themselves. New York: Feldheim Publishers, 1994. p. 13.

Text 2

THE BOY ON BUS #37

My name is Micha'el and I'm twelve. I'm in seventh grade and I live in Jerusalem, in Rehavia.

WALDER, Chaim. *Kids Speak 3:* Children Talk about Themselves. New York: Feldheim Publishers, 1997. p. 37.

a To talk about themselves, the children use "My name _____" and "I _____".

☐ am/is   ☐ is/'m (am)

b The negative form of "I'm" is…

☐ any way.   ☐ I'm not.

2 Circle the appropriate options to make true sentences about yourself. Then introduce yourself to a partner using these sentences as examples.

a My name **is/is not** Ze'ev.
b I **am/am not** twelve years old.
c **I'm/I'm not** in seventh grade. I **am/am not** in sixth grade.
d **I'm/I'm not** special.

> **Useful language**
> How old are you?
> I'm eleven years old.

3 Do you know these characters? Read about them. Then circle the appropriate options.

Text 3

DEE DEE IS DEXTER'S TROUBLESOME SISTER.

Available at <https://www.giantbomb.com/cartoon-network/3025-1737/characters/>. Accessed on February 15, 2019.

Text 4

THE MINIONS ARE SMALL, CYLINDRICAL, YELLOW CREATURES WHO HAVE ONE OR TWO EYES.

Available at <http://despicableme.wikia.com/wiki/Minions>. Accessed on February 15, 2019.

a In text 3, the form of the verb "to be" is **are/is**.
b In text 4, the form of the verb "to be" is **are/is**.
c **Are/Is** is used in text 3 because "Dee Dee" is a **singular/plural** noun; and **are/is** is used in text 4 because "Minions" is a **singular/plural** noun.

4 Look at texts 1-4 again and complete the chart.

Personal pronouns	To be	Contracted form	Examples
I	am	___	I'm in fifth grade.
He/She/It	___	's	Dee Dee (She) is Dexter's sister. My name (It) is Ze'ev.
We/You/They	___	're	The Minions (They) are small, cylindrical, yellow creatures.

5 Observe the use of *not* in "*I'm not really special*", in text 1. Following this rule, what is the negative form of *is* and *are*?

_____

6 Now observe: *I am = I'm; I am not = I'm not*. By deduction, what is the short form for *she is not, they are* and *they are not*?

_____

7 Look at the sentences. What happens to the subject and the verb *to be* in interrogative sentences? Check.

> Who **is** Dee Dee? She **is** Dexter's sister.
> Who **are** they? They **are** the Minions.

a **Verb** and <u>subject</u> change position. ☐

b The **verb** stays in the same place. ☐

c The **verb** goes to the end of the sentence. ☐

8 Based on activity 7, complete the chart.

Negative form	Interrogative form
I ___ not ('m not)	___ I?
He/She/It ___ not ('s not) (isn't)	___ he/she/it?
We/You/They are ___ ('re not) (aren't)	___ we/you/they?

Sync Listening: This is me

Pre-listening

1 Nalinkarn is a student from Thailand. She is introducing herself. What pieces of information do you think she includes in her introduction? Check.

a ☐ her name　　　　　　e ☐ her best friend's name
b ☐ her nickname　　　　f ☐ her favorite hobbies
c ☐ her nationality　　　g ☐ her favorite sports
d ☐ her age　　　　　　　h ☐ her favorite color

Listening

2 🎧 8 Listen to the audio and check your answers in activity 1.

3 🎧 8 Listen to the audio again and put the topics (hobbies and sports) in the order you hear them. The first one is done for you.

sailing

listening to music

drawing

watching movies

reading novels

playing sports

badminton

horseback riding

basketball

swimming

4 🎧 9 Listen to people from different countries. Where do they come from? Number the countries in the order you hear them.

☐ Brazil　　☐ Australia　　☐ Japan　　☐ Turkey　　☐ Ireland

5 🎧 10 Listen to three extracts from Nalinkarn again. Compare the way she pronounces the words in bold to the way the speakers in activity 4 do it. Is it different or similar?

"I'm an only **child** […]"　　"[…] Reading **novels** […]"　　"[…] And **watching** movies."

Post-listening

6 When you talk about yourself, do you mention the same things Nalinkarn does?

L3

Sync Speaking: My presentation

Pre-speaking

1 Answer the questions about yourself. Then share your answers with your classmates.

a How do you usually feel when you have to introduce yourself to other people?

☐ I feel OK.
☐ I feel nervous.
☐ I feel a bit uncomfortable.
☐ I feel anxious.

b What do you think is important for a successful formal presentation?

☐ To speak clearly.   ☐ To be different.
☐ To choose interesting topics.   ☐ To be funny.
☐ To be serious.   ☐ To improvise.
☐ To be or sound natural.

2 Prepare a self-presentation. Follow the instructions.

a Write a paragraph about yourself. Include: your first name, surname, nickname (if you have one), age, school grade, hobbies and interests.
b Read your paragraph aloud to a classmate.
c Ask for feedback.
d Revise your text.

> **Useful language**
> How you can react to your classmates' presentations:
> Well done!
> Very good!
> How interesting!
> Wow!
> Sorry, can you repeat that, please?

Speaking

3 Form a group and make your presentation.

Post-speaking

4 Discuss these questions with your classmates.

a Based on your classmates' presentations, what do you have in common with them? Check.

☐ name   ☐ nickname
☐ surname   ☐ hobbies
☐ age   ☐ interests
☐ school grade   Other: _____

b Are you ready for a future opportunity to introduce yourself in English?

Studio Scrapbook

> **What:** a scrapbook
> **To whom:** for personal use; other students
> **Media:** paper; digital
> **Objective:** organize a visual presentation

Language clue

A **scrapbook** is a book of blank pages for sticking pictures, drawings, cuttings, stickers etc. Scrapbooks help us tell a story, keep good memories etc.

1. Make a list of things to include in your scrapbook.
2. Look for pictures that represent your identity.
3. Write captions for the pictures collected. Use different letters, fonts and colors.
4. Put the captions and pictures on the page.
5. Share your work with a classmate.
6. Ask for and give feedback as well.
7. Revise your text.
8. Organize the pictures and the texts in your scrapbook.
9. Share your work with your classmates. Invite other people to see it.
10. Publish your work on the **Students for PEACE Social Media** <www.studentsforpeace.com.br>, using the tag **scrapbook** or others chosen by the students.

Peace talk

Chapters 1 and 2
We all are one

1 Read the song lyrics. Then answer: is it about children only or about humans in general?

We All Are One

1 We all are one, we are the same person
2 I'll be you, you'll be me (Oh, yeah)
3 We all are one, same universal world
4 I'll be you, you'll be me

5 No matter where we are born,
6 We are human beings
7 The same chemistry
8 Where emotions and feelings
9 All corresponding in love
10 Compatible

11 You can't get around it,
12 No matter how hard you try
13 You better believe it
14 And if you should find out
15 That you are no different than I
16 Reply

Chorus

17 The only difference I can see
18 Is in the conscience
19 And the shade of our skin doesn't matter,
20 We laugh, we chatter, we smile
21 We all live for

22 And the feelings that make
23 All those faces always renew
24 So true, so true
25 And would you believe that I have
26 All those same feelings too
27 The same as you

Chorus

28 Look at the children
29 They're having fun, with no regards to why
30 They all look different but deep inside
31 Their feelings of love they don't hide, they don't hide
32 They don't hide, they don't hide

Chorus

"We All Are One". Written by: Amir S. Bayyan, Huey P. Harris, Joseph Ellis Williams and Raymond Harris. Performed by: Jimmy Cliff. *The Power and the Glory*.
© Universal Music Publishing Group. 1983.

2 Match each argument to its corresponding numbered line in the song.

a A letra da canção afirma que todos/as nós somos seres humanos. _____

b O local onde nascemos não tem importância. _____

c Os autores dizem que temos a mesma composição química. _____

d A canção diz que a cor da nossa pele não importa. _____

e Fazemos as mesmas coisas: rimos, batemos papo, sorrimos. _____

f Os autores afirmam que as crianças se divertem sem ter um motivo. _____

g As crianças não escondem seu sentimento de amor. _____

3 Work on item "a" on your own. Then work in groups. Follow the instructions.

a A letra da canção menciona várias características que os humanos têm em comum. Liste outras semelhanças entre você e as pessoas com quem você se relaciona, além das citadas na canção.

_____

b Em grupos, compare sua lista com as de seus/suas colegas. Há semelhanças que vocês não listaram? Em sua opinião, por que elas não foram incluídas? Você concorda com as ideias de outros membros do grupo? Por quê?

c Quais semelhanças mais se repetiram nas listas? Com base nisso e na letra da canção, você concorda que todos/as nós somos iguais, apesar de nossas diferenças individuais? Por quê?

4 Discuss these questions with your classmates.

a Que tipo de sociedade podemos ajudar a construir com o exercício de nos ver na outra pessoa, de entender que ele/ela é igual a cada um/uma de nós em muitos aspectos?

b Que atitudes diárias podem mostrar nossa disposição em tratar outras pessoas da forma como gostaríamos de ser tratados/as?

5 Create a collage to represent the message that the song "We All Are One" conveys. Follow the instructions.

a Em grupos, recorte imagens de revistas usadas e faça uma colagem representando a ideia de que "todos somos um". Crie algo para encorajar as pessoas a não julgar as outras segundo padrões inventados pela sociedade, a respeitar as crianças, os/as idosos/as, as pessoas com necessidades especiais e as minorias, a ter uma atitude positiva para com a vida etc.

b Escreva legendas em inglês (e em outras línguas que você conheça) para descrever o que as imagens mostram ou expressar a sua ideia de alguma forma.

c Faça uma exposição dos trabalhos nos murais da escola e convide a comunidade para participar.

Prinsa S. (13 years old). *The World of Peace and Harmony*. Kathmandu, Nepal. Available at <http://www.unartforpeace.org/e/6153>. Accessed on May 19, 2019.

3 Family

Characters from the TV series *Everybody Hates Chris*. 2005-2009. Pictured (clockwise from top): Drew, Gene, Julius, Tonya, Rochelle and Chris

Goals
- Interview someone in order to make an oral presentation.
- Learn vocabulary for family members.
- Listen to people talk about family relationships.
- Read and create comic strips about families.
- Review the genitive case ('s) to describe family relationships.
- Understand and create a family tree.
- Understand the use of possessive adjectives and pronouns.

 **Look at the pictures and do the activities.**

a What do the pictures show? Check the appropriate boxes.

	bike	boy	family	girl	laptop	man	TV set	woman
1								
2								
3								
4								

Scene from the movie *Despicable Me 2* (2013). Pictured: Gru (left) and his adopted children (clockwise from top) Edith, Agnes and Margo

Segunda classe (1933), by Tarsila do Amaral. Oil on canvas, 110 x 151 cm. Private collection, São Paulo, Brazil

Família (1922), by Lasar Segall. Watercolor and gouache on paper, 44.8 x 43.7 cm. Museu Lasar Segall, São Paulo, Brazil

b Are these statements *T* (true) or *F* (false)?

- [ ] The woman (Rochelle) in picture 1 is probably the mother of the family.
- [ ] The family in picture 1 is not a happy family.
- [ ] The people in picture 2 do not form a family.
- [ ] Apparently, the family in picture 3 is not rich.
- [ ] The family in picture 3 looks happy.
- [ ] The family in picture 4 consists of only three members.
- [ ] We can say that the families in pictures 1 and 3 are big families.
- [ ] We cannot say that the families in pictures 2 and 4 are small families.

Going further

The Brazilian Child and Adolescent Statute

Read article 25 of the Brazilian Child and Adolescent Statute (Estatuto da Criança e do Adolescente – ECA). It presents two types of families. Which of those types applies to your family?

2 What about your family? Is it big or small?

L1

Explore Comic strip

Pre-reading

1 Look at the comic strips in activity 2 and answer the questions.

a Do you like reading this type of text?

_____

b Where can we find comic strips? Check all the possible options.
- [ ] In biographies.
- [ ] In comic books.
- [ ] In dictionaries.
- [ ] In comic magazines.
- [ ] In newspapers.
- [ ] On blogs.

c Why do people usually read comic strips? Check all the possible options.
- [ ] To find the meaning of words.
- [ ] To read a comic story in a more condensed format.
- [ ] To have fun.
- [ ] To read picture captions.

d Check two characteristics of a comic strip.
- [ ] It's a long story.
- [ ] It's usually made up of three or four panels.
- [ ] It contains many characters.
- [ ] It combines verbal and non-verbal language.

Reading

2 Read the texts and identify the subject of each comic strip. Then match.

Text 1 (from the *Family Tree* comic strip series)

Text 2 (from the *Mama's Boyz* comic strip series)

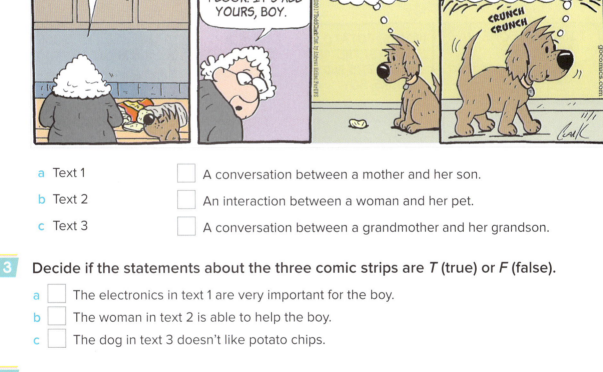

Text 3 (from the *Lola* comic strip series)

- a Text 1 ☐ A conversation between a mother and her son.
- b Text 2 ☐ An interaction between a woman and her pet.
- c Text 3 ☐ A conversation between a grandmother and her grandson.

3 Decide if the statements about the three comic strips are *T* (true) or *F* (false).

- a ☐ The electronics in text 1 are very important for the boy.
- b ☐ The woman in text 2 is able to help the boy.
- c ☐ The dog in text 3 doesn't like potato chips.

4 In texts 1 and 2, the boys use different family titles to speak to the women they are interacting with. What words do they use? Write them in the column "Word used".

	Word used	Meaning			
		mother	sister	grandmother	daughter
Text 1					
Text 2					

5 What do the words you identified in activity 4 mean? Check the appropriate answer on the chart.

L1

6 What cognates can you identify in the three comic strips? Check.

- [ ] electronics
- [ ] lunch
- [ ] Math (Mathematics)
- [ ] moment
- [ ] story
- [ ] trip
- [ ] trunk
- [ ] vital

7 What are some other characteristics of comic strips? Use the words and expressions from the box to label the elements.

> onomatopoeia panel with border panel with no border
> speech bubble thought bubble use of capital letters

TIME FOR SOME LUNCH, MAX.

WOOPS! POTATO CHIP ON THE FLOOR. IT'S ALL YOURS, BOY.

I HAVE MY PRIDE.

LUCKILY THIS ISN'T A MOMENT I NEED IT.

CRUNCH CRUNCH

Post-reading

8 Tell your classmates which of the comic strips presented here is your favorite. Use the sentences below as ideas for your answers.

> Number 1 is my favorite because I'm also a bit dependent on technology.

> Number 2 is my favorite because I find Math difficult too.

> Number 3 is my favorite because I like stories with animals.

Building blocks — Family members

1 Look at this family tree. Do you recognize these characters? Who are they?

Chris Rock's family tree

2 Observe other family relationships. Then circle the appropriate options.

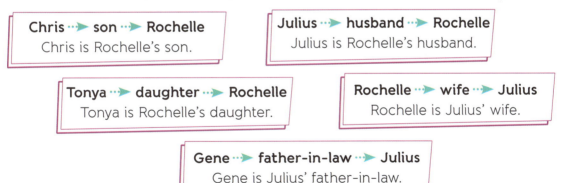

a Chris is Julius' **son/daughter/brother**.
b Chris is Tonya's **sister/brother/son**.
c Gene is Rochelle's **father-in-law/father/mother**.
d Tonya is Julius' **sister/daughter/son**.

3 Draw your own (or imaginary) family tree on a sheet of paper and share it with a partner. Then write four sentences about your family near your drawing.

L2

Toolbox Possessive adjectives/Review the genitive case ('s)

1 Read the extract about the comic strip *Mama's Boyz*. Then answer the questions.

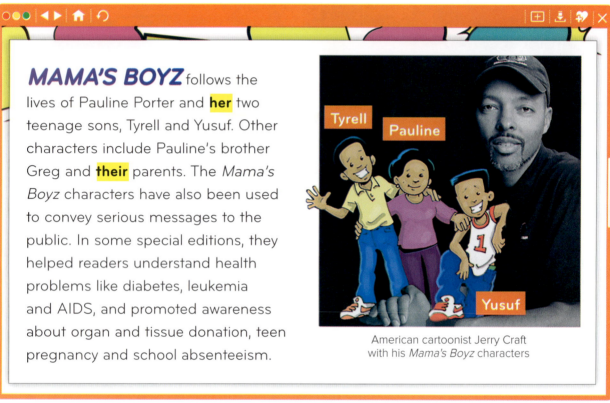

MAMA'S BOYZ follows the lives of Pauline Porter and **her** two teenage sons, Tyrell and Yusuf. Other characters include Pauline's brother Greg and **their** parents. The *Mama's Boyz* characters have also been used to convey serious messages to the public. In some special editions, they helped readers understand health problems like diabetes, leukemia and AIDS, and promoted awareness about organ and tissue donation, teen pregnancy and school absenteeism.

American cartoonist Jerry Craft with his *Mama's Boyz* characters

Adapted from <http://www.jerrycraft.net/mamasboyz.html>. Accessed on February 22, 2019.

a Who are the main characters in *Mama's Boyz*?
_____
_____

b Who are the secondary characters in *Mama's Boyz*?
_____
_____

c What words related to family members appear in the text?
_____
_____

2 Complete the sentences about the text in activity 1 using names from the box. Two names will not be used.

Pauline and Greg	Tyrell and Yusuf	Pauline

a The highlighted word "her" refers to _____.

b The highlighted word "their" refers to _____.

3 Read the sentences in these panels, taken from texts 1 and 2 of the "Explore" section. Then check the appropriate options.

a The word "our" in panel 1 refers to…
☐ the boy's trip.
☐ the boy's trip with his grandmother.

b The word "my" in panel 2 refers to…
☐ the boy's mother.
☐ the boy's homework.

c The word "your" in panel 3 refers to…
☐ the boy's brother.
☐ the boy's uncle.

> **Language clue**
>
> **aunt** = the sister of your father or mother
> **uncle** = the brother of your father or mother
> **cousin** = the son or daughter of your uncle or aunt

4 Based on the examples in activities 1, 2 and 3, complete the chart.

Possessive adjectives		
Personal pronouns	**Possessive adjectives**	**Examples**
I	_____	I have a sister. _____ sister's name is Lea.
you	_____	You have an uncle in Chile. _____ uncle's name is Diego.
_____	his	_____ has a cousin. His cousin's name is Anna.
she	_____	She has a pet. _____ pet is a cat.
_____	its	_____ is a zebra. Its colors are black and white.
we	_____	We have many cousins. _____ family is big.
you	_____	You have an aunt in Miami. _____ aunt's name is Paula.
they	_____	They have a baby. _____ baby is cute.

5 Look at the picture. Who are these characters? Label the picture.

6 Circle the appropriate possessive adjective to complete each sentence about the characters in activity 5.

a Charles Addams is the creator of *The Addams Family*. **Your/His/My** characters are very famous.

b Gomez Addams is American, but **his/her/its** parents were probably of Latin American descent.

c Cousin Itt is also a member of this family. **Our/My/Its** appearance is a bit strange.

d Morticia is a character of *The Addams Family*. **Her/His/Their** husband is Gomez Addams.

e Pugsley and Wednesday are siblings. **Her/Their/His** parents are Gomez and Morticia.

f I like *The Addams Family*. **Our/Its/My** favorite character is Grandmama Addams.

7 Rewrite the sentences as in the example.

a Gomez is the son of Grandmama Addams.
Gomez is Grandmama Addams' son.

> **Language clue**
> **sibling** = a brother or a sister

b Grandmama Addams is the mother-in-law of Morticia.

c Wednesday is the daughter of Morticia.

d Pugsley is the son of Gomez and Morticia.

Sync Listening: Interview

Pre-listening

1 How is your relationship with your family? Read the questionnaire and answer *Y* (yes) or *N* (no). Then compare your answers to a partner's.

My relationship with my family

a ☐ I have a good relationship with my parents.	f ☐ I follow all the rules in my family.
b ☐ I help with the household chores.	g ☐ We are interested in the same hobbies.
c ☐ I quarrel with my brother(s)/sister(s) a lot.	h ☐ I spend time with my family on the weekends.
d ☐ I sometimes help cook something for my family.	i ☐ I have to look after my younger sibling(s).
e ☐ We like to do things together.	j ☐ My parents put a lot of pressure on me.

Listening

2 🎧 11 Listen to four teenagers talking about their relationships with their families. Number the sentences according to what they say.

- a ☐ She has to look after her siblings.
- b ☐ Every weekend he has a family movie night.
- c ☐ When something is on her mind, she prefers to talk to her friends.
- d ☐ He thinks his parents put a lot of pressure on him.
- e ☐ He argues with his family over what movie to watch.
- f ☐ She has a sister to whom she can talk about a lot of stuff.

3 🎧 12 Now listen to an excerpt about the importance of parents in their children's education. Check the appropriate options.

a The person who answers the questions is Chris Rock's ☐ wife. ☐ mother.

b She is ☐ in a conference. ☐ at home.

c At the end of the event, she says, ☐ "Everything starts at school.". ☐ "Everything starts in the home.".

Post-listening

4 When something is on your mind, who do you usually prefer to talk to about it: a friend or a family member?

L3

Sync Speaking: Interview about your family

Pre-speaking

1 Read this excerpt from the profile of Chris Rock. What questions did the interviewer probably ask to get these pieces of information? Check.

- [ ] How do you spell "information"?
- [ ] What's your birth name?
- [ ] What are your daughters' names?
- [ ] Who's your favorite brother?
- [ ] What's your father's name?
- [ ] What's your mother's name?

CHRIS ROCK

Personal information

Birth name: Christopher Julius Rock III

Birthplace: Andrews, South Carolina, United States

Profession: comedian, actor, producer, director, screenwriter

Relationships

Julius Rock: father
Rose Rock: mother
Andre Rock: brother
Brian Rock: brother
Charles Rock: half-brother
Jordan Rock: brother
Kenny Rock: brother
Tony Rock: brother
Andrea Rock: sister
Lola Simone Rock: daughter
Zahra Savannah Rock: daughter
Malaak Compton: ex-wife

Adapted from <http://www.tvguide.com/celebrities/chris-rock/bio/144539/>. Accessed on February 22, 2019.

2 Create your own profile in your notebook. Use the text in activity 1 as an example.

Speaking

3 Time to speak. Follow the instructions and use the boxes "Useful language" to help you.

a In pairs, interview your partner. Ask questions about his/her family. Change roles.

b Plan an oral presentation for the class about your partner's family. Use the information from the interview you conducted.

Useful language

Questions	Answers
What's your/your mother's/your father's name?	My/His/Her name's… / It's…
How old are you?	I'm… (years old).
Where are you/your parents from?	I'm/They're from…
Do you have any brothers or sisters?	Yes, I do./No, I'm an only child.

Useful language

You can ask for help with vocabulary using questions like this: How can I say *sobrinha* in English?

Post-speaking

4 How are your classmates' families different from or similar to yours? Consider, for example, the number of brothers and sisters they have.

Studio Comic strip

BRAINSTORM — DRAFT — SHARE — REVISE — FINAL TEXT

> **What:** a comic strip about families
> **To whom:** school classmates
> **Media:** paper; digital
> **Objective:** create a comic strip to amuse people

1. Make a list of the elements that make up a comic strip.
2. Use your imagination and think about a funny family scene.
3. Make a sketch of the scene with the characters.
4. Decide about the visual language (hand drawing, computerized drawing, collage etc.) of your comic strip.
5. Review the sections of this chapter as well as your notes to help you with the vocabulary.
6. Share your sketch with some classmates and, if possible, with your Arts teacher.
7. Give feedback to your classmates.
8. Revise your text.
9. Make the final version of your comic strip.
10. Publish your work on the **Students for PEACE Social Media** <www.studentsforpeace.com.br>, using the tag **comicstrip** or others chosen by the students.

> **Language clue**
>
> **sketch** = a simple drawing with no details

4 School life

Salusbury World, England

Goals
- Compare different types of schools all over the world.
- Identify the days of the week, time and school subjects.
- Read and create a paragraph describing your school timetable.
- Read and create a school timetable.
- Talk about your study routine.
- Understand someone talking about homeschooling.
- Use "at", "in", "on", "from... to" with adverbs of time.
- Use the present simple affirmative to describe daily school routines.

Spark

1 Look at the pictures of different classrooms around the world. Read the descriptions and match. Write the numbers.

a A rural school in South America. There is one teacher and twelve students. The students are from 4 to 11 years old. At this school, kids milk cows, plant and cook: _____

b A primary school in Europe. It provides education and social support for refugee and migrant children: _____

c A school that offers education to kids of an indigenous community in Brazil: _____

d A school and non-profit organization in Asia. It welcomes children who are in vulnerable conditions: _____

Sateré-Mawé indigenous school, Brazil

Agustín Ferreira School, Uruguay

Mashal Model School, Pakistan

2. Compare your classroom to the classrooms in the pictures. Which one shows more similarities between them? Complete the space and circle the appropriate options.

Picture _____, because my classroom is also **big/small**; because there **are/aren't** many students in my classroom.

3. Which picture shows your favorite classroom? Why? Write the number and check the reason.

Picture _____, because it is...

☐ big ☐ colorful ☐ crowded
☐ open ☐ small Other: _____

L1

Explore Timetable

Pre-reading

1 Look at the text in this timetable. Then answer the questions.

	Monday	Tuesday	Wednesday	Thursday	Friday
7:30-7:45	Arrival/Set Up				
7:45-8:35	Math	Physics	Math	Physics	English
8:35-9:25	Math	Physics	Math	Physics	English
9:25-10:15	Social Studies	Science	Social Studies	Science	Spanish
10:15-10:45	Break				
10:45-11:35	Literature	Art	ICT	English	Music
11:35-12:25	Literature	Art	ICT	English	Music

a Where can we find this kind of text? (You can check more than one option.)

☐ In a school diary.   ☐ On a school webpage.
☐ On a school notice board.   ☐ On a report card.

b What types of information are provided?

☐ The time, the days of the week and the homework assignments.
☐ The time, the exam dates and the school subjects.
☐ The time, the days of the week and the school subjects.

Reading

2 Anna and Júlio are Brazilian students who live abroad. Read the paragraphs about their school routines, taken from an educational website, and answer the questions.

Text 1

I'm Anna and I live in Sydney (Australia) and go to Redlands School. I am in grade 6. We have classes from 8:20 a.m. to 3:20 p.m. I have Math, English, Sport, Music, Art lessons and Library lessons. I have lunch at one o'clock. We have Spanish lessons on Thursdays.

Available at <https://www.writeabout.com/2018/02/my-school-day-2/>. Accessed on March 10, 2019.

Text 2

Adapted from <https://www.writeabout.com/2018/02/me-and-my-brother-4/>. Accessed on March 10, 2019.

> **Language clue**
> The abbreviation "a.m." (*ante meridiem*) means "before midday", and "p.m." (*post meridiem*) means "after midday".

a. What is the objective of these texts?

☐ To describe a school routine. ☐ To share a school routine online.

b. Who usually reads texts like these? Check all possible answers.

☐ Students. ☐ Students' families. ☐ Teachers. ☐ Lexicographers.

c. Both texts include cognates for school subjects. Which of the school subjects in Portuguese below have equivalents in the texts? Check.

☐ Arte ☐ Estudos Sociais ☐ Literatura
☐ Ciências ☐ Física ☐ Matemática
☐ Educação Física ☐ Geografia ☐ Música
☐ Espanhol ☐ História
☐ Esporte ☐ Língua Portuguesa

d. When and where do Anna, Júlio and Carlos study? Check the periods of the day and write the places.

	Period of the day		Place
	morning	afternoon	
Anna			
Júlio			
Carlos			

> **Going further**
> Social Studies is a school subject that includes Social Sciences, such as History, Geography and Politics.

L1

3 Read this school timetable. Is it Anna's, Júlio's or Carlos'?

Text 3

Period	Time	Monday	Tuesday	Wednesday	Thursday	Friday
Roll call	8:20 - 8:30	Roll call	Roll call	Roll call	Roll call	Roll call
1	8:30 - 9:00	English WrA	Music	Math	English	Drama
2	9:00 - 9:30	English WrB	Music	Art	English	Christian Studies
3	9:30 - 10:00	Art	English	English	Spanish	English
4	10:00 - 10:30	Art	English	English	Spanish	English
Recess	10:30 - 11:00					
5	11:00 - 12:00	Math	Numeracy Groups	Math	Numeracy Groups	Library A
6	12:00 - 12:30	Math	Numeracy Groups	Math	Numeracy Groups	Library B
7	12:30 - 1:00	Chapel	Literacy Groups	UI	Literacy Groups	Math
8	1:00 - 1:30	Chapel	Literacy Groups	UI	Literacy Groups	Math
Lunch 1	1:00 - 1:30	Lunch	Lunch	Lunch 12:50-1:30	Lunch	Lunch
Lunch 2	1:30 - 1:50	Lunch	Lunch	Sport	Lunch	Lunch
9	1:50 - 2:20	UI	PE	Sport	UI	Genius Hour
10	2:20 - 2:50	UI	PE	Sport	UI	Genius Hour
11	2:50 - 3:20	UI	English	Sport	English	English
End of day	3:20					
Activities	3:30 - 4:30					

4 Read text 3 again and check the appropriate statements.

a ☐ Anna has Math on Tuesdays.
b ☐ Lunchtime is different on Wednesdays.
c ☐ Drama classes are in the afternoon.
d ☐ Recess is from 10:30 to 11:00.
e ☐ Sport classes are in the morning.
f ☐ She has English classes every day.

Post-reading

5 Which of the school subjects mentioned in the three texts do you have in your school?

6 Is there any subject mentioned in these texts that you would like to know more about? If so, which one?

L2

Building blocks Exploring a school timetable: vocabulary and time

1 Look at the timetable from Delia School of Canada, an international school in Hong Kong. Then classify the school subjects in the chart according to the areas.

		Monday	Tuesday	Wednesday	Thursday	Friday
8:00-8:15	15	Student Arrival					
8:15-8:20	5	Homeroom, Attendance and Announcements				
8:20-9:00	40	Science & Technology	Mathematics	Visual Arts	Mathematics	Science & Technology
9:00-9:40	40	Science & Technology	Mathematics	Visual Arts	Physical Education	Science & Technology
9:40-10:20	40	Music	Social Studies	Science & Technology	Mathematics	Drama or Dance
10:20-10:35	15	Recess				
10:35-11:15	40	English or ESL	International Language	International Language	International Language	International Language
11:15-11:55	40	English or ESL	Health	Music	Drama or Dance	Social Studies
11:55-12:20	25	Lunch				
12:20-12:45	25	Recess				
12:45-1:25	40	Physical Education	English or ESL	Mathematics	Social Studies	English or ESL
1:25-2:05	40	Mathematics	English or ESL	Mathematics	Social Studies	English or ESL
2:05-2:20	15	Recess				
2:20-3:00	40	Social Studies	ICT Literacy	English or ESL	English or ESL	Mathematics
3:00		Student Dismissal				

Adapted from <http://www.delia.edu.hk/upload/DSCDocument/6A.pdf>. Accessed on April 2, 2019.

Art/Culture	Languages	Sports/Well-being	Technology	Other areas

2 Now compare the timetable above to Anna's timetable on page 50. Then write *T* (true) or *F* (false).

a ☐ Anna has recess at 10:30 and Delia's students have recess at 10:20.

b ☐ Anna has Physical Education on Tuesdays and Delia's students have Physical Education on Fridays.

c ☐ Anna's classes finish at 3:20 and Delia's students' classes finish at 3:20 too.

d ☐ Roll call or attendance starts at 8:20 for Anna and at 8:15 for Delia's students.

e ☐ Anna goes to Drama class on Fridays and Delia's students go to Drama or Dance Class on Thursdays and Fridays.

L2

3 Look at the timetable in activity 1 again and find other ways to write these times.

a eight o'clock: _____

b two o-five (or) five past two: _____

c eleven fifteen (or) a quarter past eleven: _____

d one twenty-five (or) twenty-five past one: _____

e ten thirty-five (or) twenty-five to eleven: _____

f nine forty (or) twenty to ten: _____

g twelve forty-five (or) a quarter to one: _____

h eleven fifty-five (or) five to twelve: _____

4 Look at these examples taken from the texts in the "Explore" section. Focus on the highlighted words. Then complete the explanations accordingly.

a "We have classes **from** 8:20 a.m. **to** 3:20 p.m."

b "I have lunch **at** one o'clock."

c "We have Spanish lessons **on** Thursdays."

d "In the second semester I have Spanish, Math Essentials and Geography **in** the morning […]."

Watch: **Telling the time**

I The preposition used before days of the week is _____, as in item _____.

II The pair of prepositions used to indicate the beginning and the end of an activity is _____, as in item _____.

III The preposition used before a specific time is _____, as in item _____.

IV The preposition used before periods of the day is _____, as in item _____.

5 Look at the pictures and compare them. From what you can observe, when do we use the expression "o'clock" to tell the time? Check the appropriate option.

☐ When the clock shows the exact hour (no minutes).

☐ When the clock shows the hour and the minutes.

It's four twenty-five.

It's four o'clock.

Toolbox: Present simple: affirmative

1 Look at these examples taken from the texts in the "Explore" section. Then underline the appropriate options.

I "[...] I **live** in Sydney [Australia] and **go** to Redlands School."
II "My brother is Carlos and he **lives** in Winnipeg too."
III "He **goes** to River Heights School [...]."
IV "I **have** Math, English, Sport, Music, Art lessons and Library lessons."
V "We **have** Spanish lessons on Thursdays."
VI "He **has** Math, Social Studies, English, French, Health and Physical Education in the morning."
VII "School **starts** at 8:50 a.m. and **ends** at 3:30 p.m."

In the affirmative form of the present simple,

a after "I" and "we" (as well as "you" and "they"), the base form of the verb **doesn't change/changes**.

b after "he" (as well as "she" and "it"), the base form of the verb **doesn't change/changes**.

c after "he" (as well as "she" and "it"), we add **-s/-es** after verbs such as "live".

d after "he" (as well as "she" and "it"), we add **-s/-es** after verbs such as "go".

e after "he" (as well as "she" and "it"), we use the verb form **have/has**.

2 Now read about the school routine of a girl named Agustina. Underline the appropriate options.

My name is Agustina and I'm 12. I'm from Argentina. We wear a uniform to school. School **start/starts** at 8:00. We **have/has** two lessons, then we have a break, then we have one lesson, then we have one more break and after that we have two more lessons. School **finish/finishes** at 12:50. In the afternoon I have Physical Education. After PE I **do/does** my homework, **watch/watches** TV and **use/uses** my phone. On Wednesdays I **have/has** English lessons.

Adapted from <https://www.writeabout.com/2016/11/my-school-routine-3/>. Accessed on March 13, 2019.

3. In pairs, compare the school timetables in this chapter (pages 48, 50 and 51) to your school timetable. Follow the examples and use the items below to help you.

- Math (Mathematics)
- English
- Science
- Physical Education (PE)
- Art
- recess (break)
- beginning of the classes
- end of the classes (student dismissal)

Delia's students have Math every day, but we have Math on Mondays, Wednesdays and Fridays.

Anna's recess is from 10:30 to 11:00, but we have recess from 9:45 to 10:00.

4. Make a survey. Ask ten students from other classes in your school about their timetable. In pairs, decide on three questions to ask them. Use the box "Useful language" below to help you. Take notes.

Useful language

What grade are you in?
I'm in grade…

What subjects do you have on…?
I have Art, Math and Science on…

What time do you have…?
I have… at…

When do you have…?
I have… on…

5. In pairs, organize the information from activity 4. Then share your findings with your classmates. Use this "Useful language" box to help you.

Useful language

(Two) students are in grade (7).
(Five) students have (Math, Geography and PE) on (Thursdays).
(One) student has (English) at (7:40 a.m.).
(Three) students have (History) on (Wednesdays).

Sync Listening: Homeschooling

Pre-listening

1 Homeschooling is the formal education of children at home. Their parents don't send them to school. Do you know any child who is homeschooled?

Listening

2 🎧 13 **Listen to a girl named Honey talking about her homeschool routine. Underline the information you hear mentioned.**

a Honey is **10/12/13** years old.

b She usually starts off the day by **practicing piano/practicing music/reading poetry**.

c Every day she **plays the violin/studies History/reads some poetry**.

d The foreign language she learns is **Spanish/Latin/French**.

3 🎧 14 **Listen to another excerpt and write *T* (true) or *F* (false).**

a ☐ Honey's mom tells her how much she should read every day.

b ☐ Honey's mom creates a list of books for the girl. Honey should read them in the week.

c ☐ Honey can decide how much she reads a day.

d ☐ Honey's favorite book is *Augustus Caesar's World*.

e ☐ One of Honey's favorite subjects is Math.

4 🎧 15 **Now listen to one more excerpt and order the statements from 1 to 3, according to their importance for Honey. Why does she prefer homeschooling?**

☐ She can focus on the subjects she really likes.

☐ It gives her more freedom.

☐ She spends more holiday time with her family.

Post-listening

5 Honey talks about the advantages of homeschooling. In your opinion, what are the advantages of studying at a school? You can use some of the ideas below.

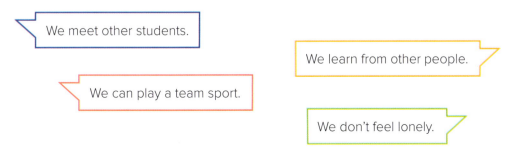

L3

Sync Speaking: Talking about your study routine

Pre-speaking

1 Read this condensed version of the audio transcription explored in the previous section. Complete it with the missing information about the girl. Then check your answers in the appendix.

Hi, guys! My name is _____ and I'm _____ years old. Today I am going to be showing you my homeschool routine. I usually start off the day by _____. Another thing I do every day is I do _____ and every day I learn _____. _____ is my favorite book that I have to read. _____ is one of my favorite subjects.

2 Plan a presentation similar to Honey's. Talk about your school routine and the things you like, using the items below as a guide. Write a draft on an extra sheet of paper.

- ▷ your name and age
- ▷ what you study in the first period (before recess)
- ▷ what subjects you study and when you have these subjects
- ▷ your favorite subject
- ▷ your favorite book

> **Useful language**
>
> My name is.../I'm...I am... years old.
> I learn (subject) on (day of the week).
> I study... in the first period (before recess).
> My favorite subject is...
> My favorite book is...

3 Show your draft to a partner and practice performing it. Ask your partner for some feedback on it. Help your partner with his/her draft and performance as well.

4 Revise your work. Rehearse your presentation in front of one or more classmates, preferably without reading.

Speaking

5 Deliver your presentation to your classmates.

> **Useful language**
>
> When you don't understand what a person said, you can say:
> *I'm sorry, I didn't understand. Can you repeat that, please?*

Post-speaking

6 Make suggestions about your classmates' presentations. How can they improve their performance next time? For example, by speaking slower? By speaking up? By using more resources, such as pictures, gestures etc.?

 **Studio** Timetable

> **What:** a timetable and a paragraph describing it
> **To whom:** for personal use; other students
> **Media:** paper; digital
> **Objective:** organize and describe your ideal timetable

1. Imagine you can choose the content for your school education. What are your favorite subjects? Make a list.
2. Draw a timetable grid. Write the days of the week and the time you want your lessons to be given.
3. Write your favorite subjects in the timetable.
4. When your ideal timetable is ready, write a paragraph describing it. Use the texts on pages 48 and 49 as examples.
5. Share your timetable and paragraph with a classmate. Read his/her work too. Give him/her some suggestions to improve it.
6. Revise your text based on your classmate's suggestions.
7. Write your final text and decorate it using your creativity.
8. Present your ideal timetable and paragraph to your class.
9. Read your classmates' productions. Are there things in common?
10. Publish your work on the **Students for PEACE Social Media** <www.studentsforpeace.com.br>, using the tag **myidealtimetable** or others chosen by the students.

_____
_____
_____
_____
_____

Peace talk

Chapters 3 and 4
Be a buddy, not a bully

1 Discuss these questions with your classmates.

    a Quando você vê ou ouve a palavra *bullying*, o que vem à sua mente?

    b Você acha que o *bullying* acontece apenas no contato direto com as pessoas da escola ou da rua? Explique.

    c Você sabe o nome que recebe o tipo de *bullying* que ocorre por meio virtual?

    d Você acha que isso só acontece com crianças e adolescentes?

2 Take a look at these posters and answer the questions.

Text 1

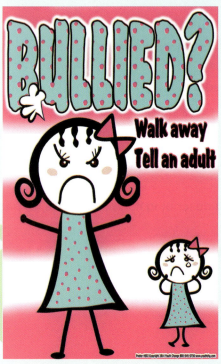

Text 2

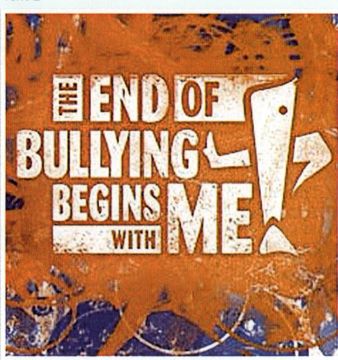

    a Qual é a mensagem de cada campanha?

    _____
    _____

    b Qual é a razão para essas campanhas existirem?

    _____
    _____

3. Look at this cartoon-poster with an example of "bullying behavior" vs. "buddy behavior". Then discuss the questions with your classmates.

a Que atitudes estão representadas no cartum?

b No primeiro quadro, como você acha que a menina deve ter se sentido? E o menino?

c No segundo quadro, como você acha que o menino à esquerda deve ter se sentido? E o outro?

d Observe como retrataram o menino que pratica *bullying*. Na sua opinião, *bullying* é comportamento só de "meninos valentões"?

4. Find stories with examples of *bullying*. Follow the instructions.

a Forme um grupo. Liste no caderno exemplos de histórias que ilustrem comportamentos de *bullying*.

b Escolha um exemplo para investigar e responda: 1. Quem são os/as protagonistas nessa situação? 2. Quais são os comportamentos de *bullying*? 3. Como a pessoa que sofreu o *bullying* se sentiu e o que aconteceu com ela? 4. O que aconteceu com quem praticou o *bullying*?

c Compartilhe suas anotações com o restante da turma. Há situações em comum? Por que escolheram esses exemplos?

d Agora, com todos os grupos juntos, escolham algumas das histórias investigadas e, para cada uma, proponham algo que pode ser considerado uma atitude camarada/amigável.

5. Create an anti-bullying campaign in your school or community. Follow the instructions.

a Forme um grupo. Escolha o conteúdo que a campanha de conscientização anti-*bullying* irá abordar.

b Pense nas ações que devem ser tomadas nessa campanha para estimular o combate ao *bullying*.

c Escolha uma data e um local para a realização da campanha.

d Produza cartazes que divulguem as atividades anti-*bullying* escolhidas.

e Exponha os cartazes nos murais da sua escola ou em locais específicos da comunidade. Lembre-se também de compartilhar seu trabalho na plataforma social da coleção.

5 Connected

Goals
- Talk about your chores at home, at school and/or in your neighborhood.
- Understand a teenager talking about her household chores.
- Understand and create memes.
- Understand the different uses of the affirmative, negative and interrogative forms of the present simple.
- Understand the use of adverbs of frequency.
- Understand the use of verbs related to household chores.

Spark

1 Look at the pictures. Then check some of the things they show.

- [ ] A ball.
- [ ] A cell phone.
- [ ] A classroom.
- [ ] A dog.
- [ ] Families.
- [ ] Teenagers.
- [ ] A timetable.
- [ ] Trash bags.
- [ ] A tablet.

2 All these expressions can describe the attitudes represented in the pictures, except one. Check the inappropriate expression.

- [ ] Sense of community.
- [ ] Sense of insecurity.
- [ ] Sense of interaction.
- [ ] Sense of responsibility.

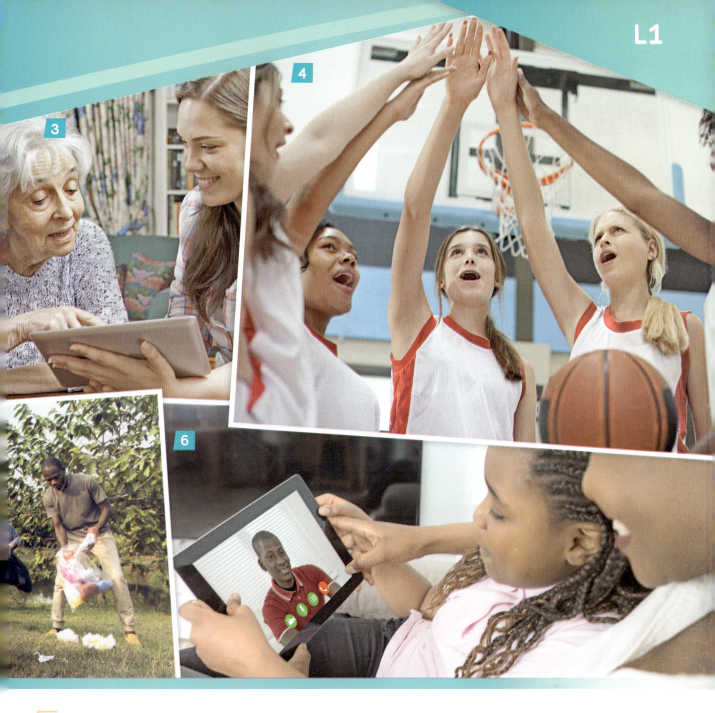

3 The pictures show possible ways people can use to **connect** with each other. How can they do it? Match the options to the appropriate pictures.

a By helping our community: _____

b By joining a team: _____

c By sharing the responsibilities at home: _____

d By teaching people new things: _____

e By using technology: _____

Going further

What does the word "connection" mean for you? Look it up in a dictionary. Then compare the dictionary definition with your opinion.

4 Do you like to connect with others?

_____

L1

Pre-reading

1 Look at the texts on the next page. Then check the appropriate options.

a ☐ These types of text are exclusively found in comic books.
b ☐ These types of text are generally anonymous.
c ☐ Texts like these often include a picture or a short video.
d ☐ Texts like these do not have verbal language (words or phrases).
e ☐ These types of text are generally humorous.
f ☐ We often find these types of text in the digital world, mainly on social media.
g ☐ These types of text are often created to share jokes, comments, emotions etc.

2 Complete the sentences about the texts in activity 4 with the appropriate numbers.

a The text(s) based on famous paintings is/are _____.

b The text(s) based on comic book characters is/are _____.

c The text(s) based on pets is/are _____.

3 What are some of the objectives of a meme? Check the appropriate options.

☐ To amuse.   ☐ To describe.
☐ To clarify.   ☐ To inform.
☐ To criticize.   ☐ To spread an idea.

> **Language clue**
> **to amuse** = to entertain, to make laugh

Reading

4 Read the four texts and underline the appropriate option in each sentence.

a Meme 1 makes use of **a definition/irony/motivational quotes**.

b Meme 2 is based on the famous painting **Abaporu, by Tarsila do Amaral/Guernica, by Pablo Picasso/The Scream, by Edvard Munch**.

c Meme 2 expresses the feeling of **courage/fear/responsibility**.

d Meme 3 is based on the famous painting **Mona Lisa, by Leonardo da Vinci/Las Meninas, by Diego Velázquez/The Dancer, by Auguste Renoir**.

e In meme 4, it is possible to say that the cat is **anxious/unhappy/happy**.

Meme 1

Meme 2

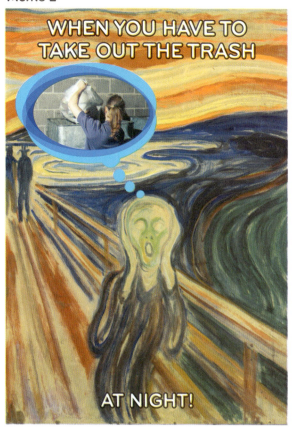

Meme 3

Meme 4

L1

5 Read the memes in activity 4 again. Then write *T* (true) or *F* (false).

a ☐ In meme 1, the child likes the idea of being a superhero.
b ☐ In meme 1, the child does the dishes every day.
c ☐ In meme 2, the person sometimes takes out the trash at night.
d ☐ In meme 2, the expression "at night!" is not essential to understand the message.
e ☐ In meme 3, the Mona Lisa parody frequently texts somebody.
f ☐ In meme 3, the Mona Lisa parody is probably frustrated.
g ☐ In meme 4, the cat symbolizes a possible human reaction.
h ☐ In meme 4, the cat doesn't want to take a selfie.

6 Read the four memes again and circle the appropriate option.

a In meme 1, the word "he" refers to the **dishes/boy**.

b In meme 2, the word "you" refers to **the reader/Edvard Munch**.

c In meme 3, the word "you" refers to the **person Mona Lisa texts with/reader**.

d In meme 3, the word "I" refers to **the person Mona Lisa texts with/Mona Lisa**.

e In meme 4, the word "your" is used to show a form of **genitive case ('s)/possession**.

> **Going further**
> The word "meme" was introduced in 1976 by British biologist Richard Dawkins in his book *The Selfish Gene*. The concept of "meme" on the web refers to humorous pictures, videos and phrases that spread rapidly by users.

Post-reading

7 Discuss this topic with your classmates.
Sometimes, memes become a problem. In which situations can this happen? Read and check.

L2

Building blocks — Household chores verbs/Adverbs of frequency

1 Look at these pictures. What do they show?

- ☐ Everyday school activities.
- ☐ Sports activities.
- ☐ Regular activities people do at home.

Watch: **Household chores**

- ○ do the dishes
- ○ take out the trash
- ○ make the bed
- ○ clear the table
- ○ sweep the floor
- ○ do the laundry
- ○ walk the dog
- ○ feed the pet (cat, dog etc.)

2 Which of the household chores in activity 1 do you do regularly? Check the pictures that apply to you.

3 Look at the percentages that some adverbs of frequency express. How often do you do the household chores listed? Check the appropriate answers for you.

Do you help around the house? How often?	ALWAYS 100%	USUALLY 90%	NORMALLY 80%	OFTEN/ FREQUENTLY 70%	SOMETIMES 50%	OCCASIONALLY 30%	SELDOM 10%	RARELY 5%	NEVER 0%
do the dishes									
do the laundry									
clear the table									
feed the pet									
make the bed									
sweep the floor									
take out the trash									
walk the dog									

L2

4 Now work with a partner and compare your answers in activity 3. Then write sentences as in the examples.

I sometimes do the dishes.

Pedro rarely does the dishes.

Pedro and I never do the laundry.

_____
_____
_____
_____
_____
_____

5 Read the memes on page 63 again. Which one includes two adverbs of frequency? What are they?

_____

6 Interview a partner. Ask him/her questions about household chores, as in the example.

> A How often do you sweep the floor?
> B Sometimes.
> A How often do you walk the dog?
> B Twice a week.

Useful language
How often do you...?
(1x) Once a day/week/month/year.
(2x) Twice a day/week/month/year.
(3x) Three times a day/week/month/year.
(4x) Four times a day/week/month/year.

7 The sentence below associates the topic of this section to the title of this chapter. Complete the sentence with the words from the box.

> always   at home   people   their

We are [_____] connected to the [_____] around us, and the work we do or do not do [_____] has an impact on [_____] lives.

8 Read the sentence in activity 7 again. Then check the option that best reflects your opinion or consideration about it.

a ☐ I completely agree.
b ☐ I partially agree.
c ☐ I disagree.
d ☐ I'm not so sure yet.
e ☐ I never think about this.
f ☐ I sometimes think about this.
Other: _____

Toolbox Present simple (affirmative, negative, interrogative)

1 What can we say about the uses of the present simple? Check.

The present simple is used to…

a ☐ express something we believe is true.
b ☐ express the frequency we do certain things.
c ☐ describe plans for the future.
d ☐ express an opinion.
e ☐ express something happening at the moment of speaking.
f ☐ describe general truths and facts.

2 Read these sentences taken from two memes on page 63. Which uses of the present simple introduced in activity 1 are observed here? Complete.

a "He **wants** to save the world, but he **doesn't want** to help do the dishes!"

b "I **don't** always **text** you, but when I **do** you never **reply**!"

In sentence "a", the present simple is used to _____.

In sentence "b", the present simple is used to _____.

3 In sentence "a", activity 2, the verb in the phrase "he doesn't want" is in…

☐ the affirmative form.   ☐ the negative form.

4 In the phrase "Do you help around the house?", on page 65, activity 3, the verb is in…

☐ the interrogative form.   ☐ the affirmative form.

5 Circle the options that make these sentences true about yourself. Then share your answers with a partner, as in the example.

a I **have/don't have** many friends in my neighborhood.

b I **think/don't think** it is important to greet the neighbors I see every day.

c I **use/don't use** social media to interact with my friends.

> Do you have many friends in your neighborhood?

> Yes, I do. I have some. (or) No, I don't either.

> No, I don't. How about you? Do you have many friends in your neighborhood?

L2

6 Look at the chart. Then complete the sentences.

Language clue
don't = do not
doesn't = does not

I text you.
You reply to me.
She walks the dog every day.
He wants to save the world.
It helps you communicate.
We make our beds.
You feed the cat.
They clear the table.

I don't text you.
You don't reply to me.
She doesn't walk the dog every day.
He doesn't want to save the world.
It doesn't help you communicate.
We don't make our beds.
You don't feed the cat.
They don't clear the table.

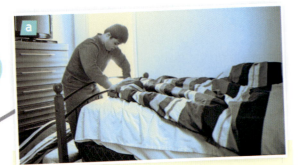

a. I usually _____ (help) around the house. I _____ (sweep) the floor and _____ (make) my bed every day, but I never _____ (take) out the trash.

b. We _____ (walk) our dogs every afternoon, but we _____ (not do) the dishes. We _____ (not like) this chore very much.

c. My older brother _____ (not like) to help around the house. He seldom _____ (do) the laundry and he never _____ (clear) the table. He _____ (text) his friends and _____ (listen) to music most of the time.

d. Kaled and Li Wei _____ (play) soccer twice a week with the school team. At home, they _____ (clean) the garage on Saturdays and _____ (do) the laundry on Fridays. They _____ (study) in the morning.

Sync Listening: My household chores

Pre-listening

1 Who helps around your house? What do people do? Complete the chart.

Who	What
Me	
My...	
My...	

2 How important do you think it is to help around the house?

☐ Very important.   ☐ Important.   ☐ Not so important.   Other: _____

Listening

3 🎧16 Listen to a girl talking about her household chores. Check the activities that you hear.

☐ Organize.   ☐ Walk the dog.   ☐ Take out the trash.
☐ Sweep the floor.   ☐ Clean the bedroom.   ☐ Do the dishes.
☐ Feed the cat.   ☐ Do the laundry.   ☐ Make the bed.

4 🎧16 Listen to the girl again and complete the sentences properly. Use the vocabulary from activity 3.

a She likes to _____.

b She doesn't like to _____.

5 🎧16 Listen again and check the reasons why she likes to do some household chores.

a ☐ Because she doesn't like to watch TV.
b ☐ Because she knows it's important to help out her family.
c ☐ Because she gets money from her parents.
d ☐ Because she loves the feeling that everything is clean.

6 🎧16 Listen one more time. What does the girl recommend trying while doing household chores? Complete.

She thinks it's a good thing to _____ because it makes it seem _____.

Post-listening

7 What do you and your classmates have in common with the girl from the audio?

L3

Sync Speaking: Talking about my chores

Pre-speaking

1 Which of the following chores do you usually do to help at your house, school or community?

- collect classwork and homework
- decorate common spaces
- erase the board
- help take care of animals
- help the elderly
- help with meals
- organize school supplies
- record classroom activities
- water plants
- work in the garden

2 Start planning a presentation about your chores. Follow the instructions.

a Think about the chores mentioned in this chapter.

b Make a list of all the chores you do at home, at school and/or in your community.

c Use a dictionary if necessary.

d Use the transcription of the audio from the previous section to help you.

e Write a text in your notebook about the chores you do.

f Use the "Useful language" box for help.

Useful language

In my…
I always…
The chores I like/don't like to do are… because…
It's a good thing if you… while you're doing it because…

Speaking

3 Practice your presentation orally. Try to speak as naturally as you can.

Post-speaking

4 Check the best options for you. Then talk to your classmates about your presentation and the preparation for it.

	easy	hard	fun	not fun
My preparation was…				
My presentation was…				

Studio Meme

> **What:** a meme
> **To whom:** other students, teachers, friends and family
> **Media:** paper; digital
> **Objective:** depict your chores with humor

1. Review this chapter and your notes. Focus on the information about memes.
2. Choose a chore that you do regularly. Use it as an inspiration for your meme.
3. Choose a picture for your meme: a photo, a drawing, a caricature etc.
4. Write the text for the meme. Remember to use just a few words.
5. Share your ideas with your classmates and listen to their suggestions.
6. Give feedback as well.
7. Revise your text.
8. Finalize your production. Consider the size and position of the picture. Think about the font size and the position of the text in your meme.
9. Share your meme with your classmates.
10. Publish your work on the **Students for PEACE Social Media** <www.studentsforpeace.com.br>, using the tag **mymeme** or others chosen by the students.

_____
_____
_____
_____
_____
_____

6 Networking

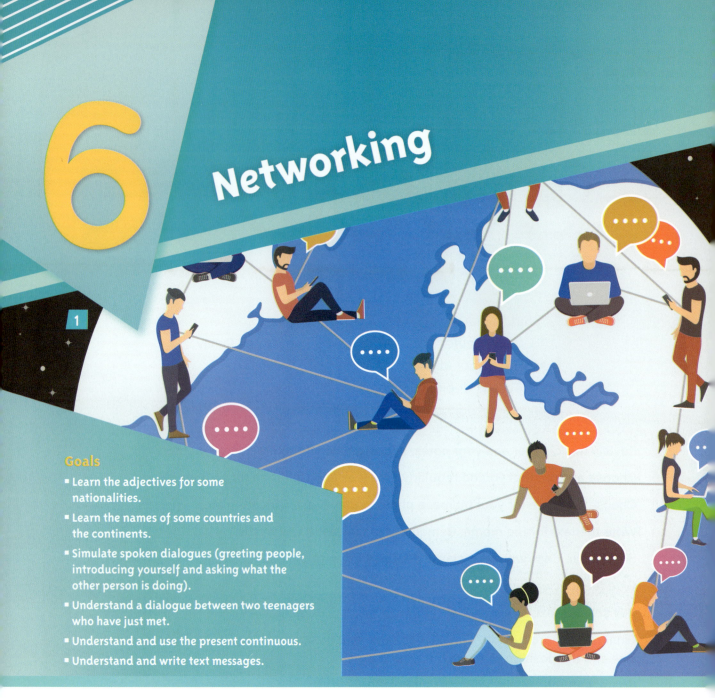

Goals
- Learn the adjectives for some nationalities.
- Learn the names of some countries and the continents.
- Simulate spoken dialogues (greeting people, introducing yourself and asking what the other person is doing).
- Understand a dialogue between two teenagers who have just met.
- Understand and use the present continuous.
- Understand and write text messages.

Spark

1 Match the descriptions to the pictures. Write the corresponding numbers.

☐ People communicating online in different parts of the world.
☐ People from different nationalities getting together.
☐ People pressing their noses together to greet each other.

2 Read the sentences and write the appropriate numbers.

a The picture that shows people from different countries waving their flags is _____.

b The picture that shows two people from different cultures greeting each other is _____.

c The picture that suggests that everybody in the world is interconnected is _____.

L1

3. Picture 2 shows a traditional way to greet people physically in New Zealand. How do people greet each other physically in your culture? Check.

☐ They shake hands.
☐ They hug.
☐ They fist bump.
☐ They kiss on the cheeks.
☐ Other: _____

Watch:
Greeting people

4. Besides the gesture in picture 2 (the *hongi*, a traditional Maori greeting), what other ways of greeting someone in other cultures do you know? Research and share your findings with your classmates.

73

L1

Explore Text message

Pre-reading

1 Look at the texts in activity 2. Do you use this type of messaging app? If so, what for? Check all answers that apply to you.

- ☐ To talk about my life.
- ☐ To ask for information.
- ☐ To ask where a friend/family member is.
- ☐ To talk about school homework.
- ☐ To invite friends for parties.
- ☐ To order food.
- ☐ To talk about sports or video games.
- ☐ Other: _____

Reading

2 Read the two texts. The first one is related to the TV series *Sam & Cat* and the second one is a scene from the movie *Raising the Bar*. Check the most appropriate options.

Text 1

Available at <http://samandcat.wikia.com/wiki/File:Sam_and_Cat_texting_promotional_image_for_pilot_premiere.jpg>.
Accessed on March 27, 2019.

> **Language clue**
>
> "Kk" in an English text message means "It is OK".
> In Portuguese, it means laughter.

Text 2

Kelly (Kelli Berglund) texting on her phone in a scene from the 2016 movie *Raising the Bar*

a In text 1, Cat is asking Sam...
- [ ] if they are watching TV together later.
- [ ] what she is doing.

b In text 1, non-verbal language is used...
- [ ] by Sam only.
- [ ] by Cat only.
- [ ] by both Sam and Cat.

c Sam uses non-verbal language in her second message to...
- [ ] express her love for animals.
- [ ] substitute a word with a symbol/picture.

d In text 2, Kelly is texting...
- [ ] her brother.
- [ ] her father.

e Kelly informs him that...
- [ ] she has her luggage with her.
- [ ] she arrived well.

f In text 2, the non-verbal language used expresses that...
- [ ] everything was fine.
- [ ] Kelly got her suitcases back.

Going further

Sam & Cat is an American TV series starring Jennette McCurdy (Sam) and Ariana Grande (Cat). The two characters become best friends after Sam saves Cat from an accident. They are roommates and work as babysitters.

Raising the Bar is an American movie that tells the story of Kelly (Kelli Berglund), a teenager that quits an elite gymnastics program in the United States and moves to Australia.

L1

3 Read texts 1 and 2 again and answer the questions.

a What is a formal way to write the question "R we watching our show together tonight?"? Who asks this question?

b Who does the word "we" in "R we watching our show together tonight?" refer to?

c In text 2, what word indicates that Kelly arrived at her destination with someone else?

d Which word do we include to write the sentences "Hey, Dad, arrived." and "Lost our suitcases." in a formal way? Rewrite them.

e In text 2, does Kelly express her opinion about the place she is in? If so, what is it?

Post-reading

4 In texts 1 and 2 people communicate using short messages. Why do they do it? Check three possible reasons and add other reasons if you wish.

☐ They need to save space.
☐ They need to write quickly.
☐ They want to confuse readers.
☐ They want to be informal.
☐ Other: _____

5 In which of these situations it is inappropriate to use informal writing? Check all possible options.

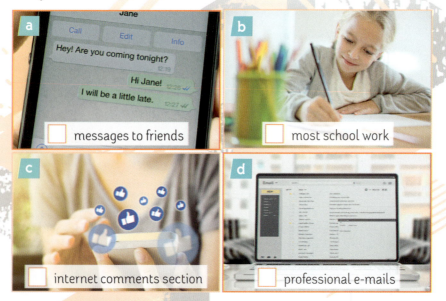

a ☐ messages to friends
b ☐ most school work
c ☐ internet comments section
d ☐ professional e-mails

L2

Toolbox Present continuous

1 Look at the text. Then check the picture that best represents the sentence "Alice is typing a message...".

2 Now look at these pictures and underline the appropriate options.

I    II

a The pictures show **internet links/status bars/play buttons**.

b The processes represented in the pictures are **finished/not finished/blocked**.

3 Look at this other text and answer the questions.

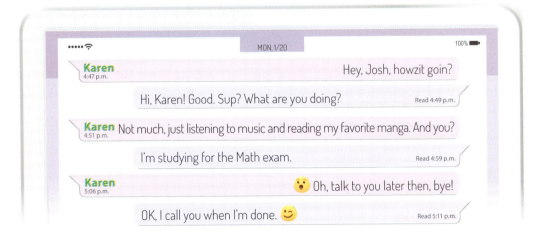

a What kind of text is this? Who takes part in it?

b What are they doing?

L2

4 What do texts in activities 1 and 3, plus the pictures in activity 2, have in common? Check.

☐ They are all related to text messages.

☐ They all mention actions happening at the moment of speaking or writing.

5 Look at the texts and pictures in activities 1, 2 and 3 again. Underline the appropriate options to complete the sentences.

a The verbs "go", "load", "download", "do", "listen", "read" and "study" received the ending *-ing/-ed*.

b The ending of these verbs in the texts and in the pictures indicates that the actions **happen frequently/are happening now**.

6 Based on the sentence "I'm studying for the Math exam.", in activity 3, we can conclude that the affirmative form of the present continuous is...

☐ subject + auxiliary verb "do" + main verb ending in *-ing*.

☐ subject + auxiliary verb "be" + main verb ending in *-ing*.

7 Now look at this extract from the text in activity 3. Focus on the highlighted sentence and check all the statements that are true about it.

> Hi, Karen! Good. Sup? **What are you doing?** Read 4:49 p.m.

a ☐ It is about an action that is in progress at the moment.
b ☐ It is about an action that usually happens.
c ☐ It is a sentence in the affirmative form.
d ☐ It is a sentence in the interrogative form.
e ☐ The auxiliary verb "be" is placed after the subject ("you").
f ☐ The auxiliary verb "be" is placed before the subject ("you").
g ☐ It is a question that requires specific information as an answer.
h ☐ It is a question that requires "yes" or "no" as an answer.

8 Think about some of your friends or family members. Then tell your classmates what you think these people are doing now. You can choose actions from the box.

cook	do homework	listen to music
play soccer	play video games
sleep	talk on the phone
walk the dog	watch TV	work

> I think my sister is walking the dog now, my grandpa is cooking, my...

Useful language

You can ask for more information or explanation during a lesson with these questions:
So, what you are saying is that...?
I don't understand. Are you saying that...?

L2

Building blocks Countries, nationalities and continents

1 Look at the two pictures and complete the sentences.

Kelly (Kelli Berglund) in a scene from the 2016 movie *Raising the Bar*

a The name of Kelly's new city is _____.

b Kelly moved to another country. She moved to _____. Someone who was born in this country is called _____.

2 "Australia", "Australian" and "Brazil", "Brazilian" are examples of countries and nationalities. What other countries and nationalities in English do you know? Classify these words by writing *C* for countries and *N* for nationalities.

☐ Indian	☐ Turkish	☐ Turkey
☐ Argentine/Argentinian	☐ Venezuela	☐ India
☐ Canada	☐ Argentina	☐ Jamaica
☐ United States of America	☐ Iraq	☐ Ugandan
☐ Cuban	☐ Iraqi	☐ Afghan/Afghani
☐ Denmark	☐ Lebanon	☐ Venezuelan
☐ Jamaican	☐ Cuba	☐ China
☐ Guatemala	☐ Chinese	☐ Taiwan
☐ Ecuadorian	☐ Canadian	☐ Afghanistan
☐ American	☐ Taiwanese	☐ Philippines
☐ New Zealander	☐ Guatemalan	☐ Peruvian
☐ Filipino	☐ Thailand	☐ Madagascar
☐ France	☐ Thai	☐ Uganda
☐ French	☐ Peru	☐ New Zealand
☐ Danish	☐ Malagasy	
☐ Ecuador	☐ Lebanese	

L2

3 Read the sentences about some famous people. Can you guess the countries they are from based on the flags and nationalities?

a. Alexis Sánchez is from _____. He is a Chilean soccer player.

b. Florinda Meza is from _____. She is a Mexican actress and producer.

c. Yoko Ono is from _____. She is a Japanese multimedia artist.

d. Malala Yousafzai is from _____. She is a Pakistani activist.

e. Seu Jorge is from _____. He is a Brazilian singer and actor.

f. Ama Ata Aidoo is from _____. She is a Ghanaian writer.

g. Greta Thunberg is from _____. She is a Swedish activist.

h. Pedro Almodóvar is from _____. He is a Spanish movie director.

4 How well do you know the continents and their countries? Draw a chart like this in your notebook and complete it with the countries mentioned in this section.

Africa	America			Asia	Europe	Oceania
	Central America	North America	South America			

Sync Listening: Meeting a new friend

Pre-listening

1 Look at the picture and make predictions about the content of the audio: Do you think the girls already know each other? What are they talking about? Where are they?

A scene from the 2016 movie *Raising the Bar*. Pictured (left to right): Nicola (Lili Karamalikis) and Kelly (Kelli Berglund)

Listening

2 🎧 17 Kelly is a new student at a school in Australia. Listen to her talking to another girl. Complete each sentence.

a Nicola's nickname is _____.

b Kelly is _____.

c Kelly moved to Australia with her _____.

3 🎧 17 Listen to the extract again and underline the appropriate options.

a Nicola introduces herself saying **only her name/her name and nickname**.

b Nicola **likes Kelly's accent/doesn't understand what Kelly says**.

c The answer to the question "Where are you from?" is **I'm from Atlanta/I was born in Atlanta**.

d Kelly says "I don't really have any friends." Then Nicola reacts saying **Well, now you do./That's so sad**.

Post-listening

4 One of the things Nicola mentions in the audio is Kelly's American accent. Discuss this topic. Read the statements and choose one of the three answers to react to each statement.

> I agree.   I agree in part.   I don't agree.

a It is important to know that there are different ways to speak English and that there isn't an "ideal" accent. _____

b Some people make fun of other people's accents. This attitude is not nice and it should be avoided. _____

L3

Sync Speaking: Greeting someone

Pre-speaking

1 How would you greet different people in English? Read the options and decide if you would use them to greet a friend (*F*), a teacher (*T*) or a family member (*FM*).

- [ ] Hi.
- [ ] Hello.
- [ ] Good morning.
- [ ] Hey.
- [ ] How's it going?
- [ ] Whazzup?
- [ ] Sup?
- [ ] Yo!
- [ ] What's new?
- [ ] What's going on?
- [ ] How are you?
- [ ] How's life?
- [ ] How have you been?
- [ ] How do you do?
- [ ] Howdy?

Speaking

2 Time to speak. Use the contexts below or think of other situations. Plan the dialogues and practice them. Then present the dialogues to the class.

a You are walking down the street. You see a friend. Greet him/her and tell him/her about what you are doing at the moment.

b Your teacher is talking to a foreigner who is visiting your school. Greet your teacher and then the visitor. Introduce yourself in English.

Useful language

Ways to respond back to greetings
Nothing much./Not much.
I'm fine./I'm doing good./
I'm OK./Fine, thanks.

Ways to introduce yourself
My name is.../I'm..., but everyone calls me...
Nice to meet you./Nice to meet you too.

Ways to say goodbye
Goodbye./Bye./See you later./
Take care.

Post-speaking

3 Some people may get angry or offended depending on the way someone else greets them. Based on this, how important do you think it is to learn this type of social skill?

Studio: Text message

BRAINSTORM — DRAFT — SHARE — REVISE — FINAL TEXT

> **What:** a text message
> **To whom:** a friend, a family member or a teacher
> **Media:** digital
> **Objective:** send a message to greet someone and talk about what is going on in your life

1. Look back at this chapter. Reflect: why do people write text messages? Can we use abbreviations? Can we include pictures?
2. Check your notes about this chapter. Find ways to greet people and verbs we can use to talk about actions.
3. Choose a person to write to.
4. Plan your text message: include some news and a question about his/her life or action at the moment.
5. Write your draft. Then share it with a classmate and ask for feedback. Do the same with his/her text.
6. Revise your text. Consider your classmate's suggestions to improve it.
7. Write your final text message.
8. Check if it is possible to send your message to the person of your choice.
9. Publish your work on the **Students for PEACE Social Media** <www.studentsforpeace.com.br>, using the tag **textmessage** or others chosen by the students.

Peace talk

Chapters 5 and 6
Building social skills

1 **Read the situations. Then check the answer that is true for you.**

a Um/a colega de sala envia uma mensagem para você dizendo que não gostou das imagens que você escolheu para o trabalho em grupo. Você...

I ☐ se irrita porque o/a colega não considerou o tempo que você gastou; você responde em letras maiúsculas que não vai procurar mais nada.

II ☐ conversa pessoalmente com ele/ela para saber que tipo de imagem você poderia procurar e tenta entender por que as imagens que você escolheu não servem.

b Um/a amigo/a está agindo de forma estranha contigo e você desconhece a razão. Você...

I ☐ se chateia e passa a tratá-lo/a da mesma forma que está sendo tratado/a.

II ☐ explica para ele/ela como você se sente e pergunta o que aconteceu.

2 **Discuss the situations in activity 1 with a partner through the following questions.**

a Quantas respostas "I" e quantas respostas "II" você marcou? Que atitudes são ilustradas nas respostas "I" e nas respostas "II"?

b Você já passou por situações semelhantes? Se sim, como lidou com elas?

"You can't be human all by yourself, and when you have this quality – *Ubuntu* – you are known for your generosity. We think of ourselves far too frequently as just individuals, separated from one another, whereas you are connected and what you do affects the whole World."

MATHEWS-AYDINLI, Julie (Ed.). *International Education Exchanges and Intercultural Understanding:* Promoting Peace and Global Relations. Ankara: Palgrave Macmillan, 2017.

3 **Read this quote by Desmond Tutu. Then answer the questions orally.**

a De acordo com a citação, o que significa ter a qualidade *Ubuntu*?

b Você considera as respostas "II" na atividade 1 exemplos da prática da filosofia *Ubuntu*? Justifique.

4 Read this text. Then discuss the questions with a partner.

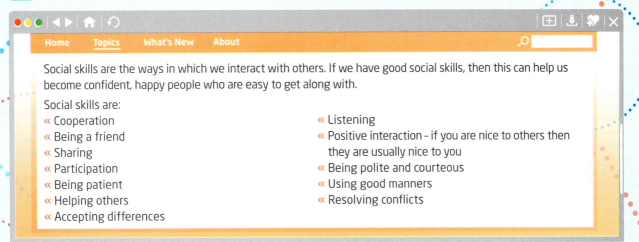

Social skills are the ways in which we interact with others. If we have good social skills, then this can help us become confident, happy people who are easy to get along with.

Social skills are:
- Cooperation
- Being a friend
- Sharing
- Participation
- Being patient
- Helping others
- Accepting differences
- Listening
- Positive interaction – if you are nice to others then they are usually nice to you
- Being polite and courteous
- Using good manners
- Resolving conflicts

Adapted from <http://www.cyh.com/HealthTopics/HealthTopicDetailsKids.aspx?p=335&np=287&id=2905>. Accessed on May 20, 2019.

a O que você entende por "*social skills*"? O texto lido pode ajudá-lo/a responder.

b Em sua opinião, essas "*social skills*" podem indicar que uma pessoa possui a qualidade *Ubuntu*? Explique.

5 Create a list of attitudes in your notebook. Follow the instructions.

a Escolha uma das *social skills* apresentadas na atividade 4 e faça uma lista de atitudes que demonstrem essa habilidade na prática.

b Ao longo da semana, observe as suas interações e as de outras pessoas em ambientes como a escola, sua casa, as redes sociais, os meios de transporte, programas de TV etc. Em quais momentos você ou outras pessoas recorreram à habilidade social que você escolheu?

c Forme um grupo. Compartilhem suas anotações. Separem as interações em duas categorias: as que foram tranquilas e as que geraram conflitos.

d Avaliem o que contribuiu para que as situações acontecessem dessa forma. Quais mudanças de comportamento devem ser consideradas para que, das próximas vezes, as interações conflituosas sejam pacíficas?

6 Create a bookmark. Follow the instructions.

Make a better world:
- Cooperate.
- Share.
- Be patient.
- Accept differences.

a Forme um grupo. Organizem-se para produzir marcadores de livros (de cartolina, EVA ou qualquer outro material disponível).

b Elaborem mensagens para encorajar a prática do *Ubuntu* no cotidiano. Pensem, por exemplo, em mensagens sobre como evitar conflitos e estimular a cooperação, o respeito e a tolerância.

c Escrevam as mensagens nos *bookmarks*, usando sua criatividade visual.

d Distribuam os *bookmarks* para promover uma campanha de conscientização *Ubuntu*. Se possível, expandam a campanha, distribuindo os marcadores para outras turmas ou mesmo presenteando outra(s) escola(s) próxima(s) à sua.

7 Sports

Goals
- Learn the names of body parts.
- Learn the use of the imperative.
- Reflect on the importance of practicing sports in order to maintain a healthy lifestyle.
- Understand and create a poster about sports and health.
- Understand and do a survey on sports and health.
- Understand and use words related to sports.
- Use the imperative to make recommendations.

Spark

1. Check the pictures that, in your opinion, are related to sports.

2. Use the words in the box to label the pictures. Then share your answers with a partner.

   | concentration | dance | energy | friendship | inclusion | sleep |

3. Which picture did you like most? Write the number and check the reason.

   Picture _____ because...

   ☐ it shows a sport or an activity I like.   ☐ it represents something important.
   ☐ Other: _____

4 Interview four classmates and complete the chart.

	How important are sports for you?				
	Classmates' names				
Answers	not important				
	important				
	very important				

5 Share your findings with the class. What do most of your classmates say about the importance of sports for them?

L1

Pre-reading

 Look at the posters (texts 1 and 2) and do these activities.

a What types of posters are these? Check all possible options.

POSTER	advertising	educational	event	motivational	movie	political	travel
1							
2							

b All of these elements can make up the types of poster seen here. Look for them in the two texts and write "1", "2" or "both". If the element is absent, write "none".

I information about place (address, city etc.): _____

II use of pictures: _____

III presence of a title: _____

IV use of different colors: _____

V use of different fonts in different sizes: _____

VI information about time: _____

VII information about dates (day of the week, month etc.): _____

VIII summary of the event: _____

IX information about prices: _____

X information about contact (phone number, website etc.): _____

XI use of a question to grab the reader's attention: _____

c In general, why do people create posters? Check all possible options.

☐ To inform people.   ☐ To sell a service or product.
☐ To amuse people.   ☐ To tell a story.

Text 1

Available at <https://i.pinimg.com/736x/9c/02/da/9c02da3b80d71c9c890a88ca37c4738c--don-t-wait-mumbai.jpg>. Accessed on June 25, 2019.

Text 2

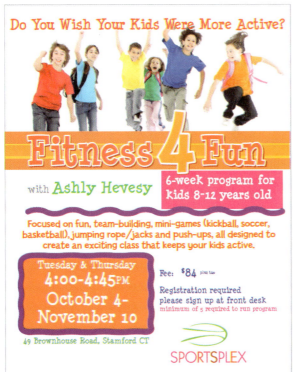

Language clue

kickball = a game similar to baseball, played with a large rubber ball that is kicked, and not hit with a bat

Available at <http://www.sportsplex-ct.com/fitness-4-fun-6-week-program-for-kids-8-12-years>. Accessed on June 25, 2019.

Reading

2 Read text 1. What can we say about it? Check all possible options.

☐ It is a poster for a campaign about good health.
☐ Its purpose is to motivate people to practice sports.
☐ A private sports center produced this poster.
☐ Its visual elements help to communicate the message.

3 Answer the questions about text 1.

a What are the two instructions that express the importance of drinking water?

_____

b Who produced this poster?

_____

4 Read text 2 and check the appropriate options.

a The text does not mention who produced it, but we can infer this information from its objective. It was probably produced by...

☐ a community center or a private sports center.   ☐ a television station.
☐ a public school.

b The question in red at the top of the poster is probably addressed to...

☐ teachers.   ☐ kids' friends.
☐ parents or adults responsible for kids.

L1

5 Answer the questions about text 2.

a What's the name of the program?
___

b What's the name of the person who will lead the program?
___

c When does the program take place?
___

d What are the programmed activities?
___

6 Now write *T* (true) or *F* (false) according to text 2.

a ☐ The program costs only $84, and no extra cost.
b ☐ Kids who are over twelve years old cannot participate.
c ☐ It is necessary to register online to participate in the program.
d ☐ You can participate if you are free on Tuesdays and Thursdays from 4 to 5 o'clock in the afternoon.
e ☐ If only four kids register, the program will not take place.

Post-reading

7 Answer these questions about the texts you have read.

a Did any of the texts teach you something new? If so, which one?
___

b Do you see texts like these in your community? If so, in what places?
___

c Do you think it is important to be physically active? If so, why?
___

d Would you recommend any of the texts to someone that you know? If so, to whom and why?
___

> **Going further**
> The International Day of Sport for Development and Peace is celebrated on April 6. For more information visit <http://www.un.org/en/events/sportday>.

Building blocks Sports and parts of the body

1 Use the words in the box to label the pictures. Then listen and practice saying these words.

| baseball | capoeira | cycling | gymnastics | running | skating |
| skiing | soccer | surfing | tennis | volleyball |

2 Work with a partner to complete the sentences. Use the vocabulary from activity 1.

a _____ is a water sport.

b _____ are ball games.

c _____ is a type of martial art.

d _____ need two or more participants.

e _____ are individual sports.

L2

3 🎧19 Listen and write the letters a-f to match the sounds you hear. Then read the verbs.

4 What sports are represented in the pictures above? Write their name.

a		d	
b		e	
c		f	

5 Look at the picture and name the parts of the body using the vocabulary from the box.

arm   finger   foot   hand   head   leg   neck

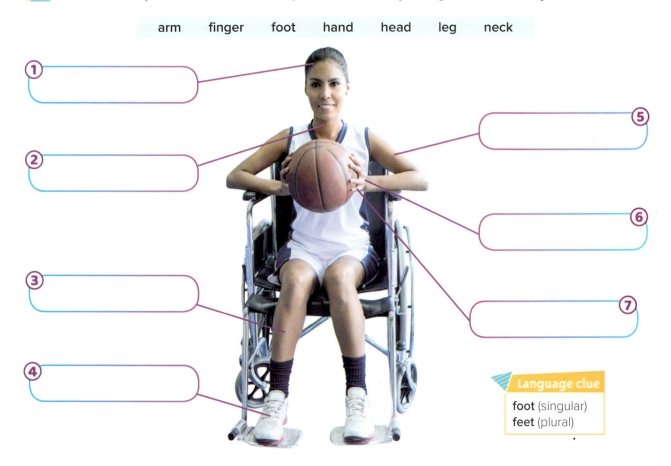

Language clue
foot (singular)
feet (plural)

6 What is your favorite sport? What parts of the body do athletes use most when practicing it? Follow the example.

My favorite sport is table tennis. Athletes use their arms and hands all the time.

---

7 "Play", "do" or "go"? Classify the sports from activity 1 in the chart.

PLAY (sports or games with ball, boards or cards)	DO (recreational activities or non-team sports that do not use a ball)	GO (sports and activities ending in -ing)

8 In pairs, practice asking and answering questions as in the example.

A Do you like sports?
B Yes, I do. I play/do/go.../No, I don't.

9 Research to find out about the importance of practicing sports in order to maintain a healthy lifestyle. Present your findings to your classmates.

L2

Toolbox Imperative

1 Read these excerpts from text 1, on page 88. Which one(s) show(s) recommendations? Check.

- [ ] Summer Tips
- [ ] Dr L H Hiranandani Hospital
- [ ] HYDRATE, HYDRATE, HYDRATE.
- [ ] Don't wait until you're thirsty to drink water. Drink plenty of water before, during and after activities.

2 What are the main verb forms in the sentences you checked in activity 1? Write them down.

_____

3 Now choose the appropriate options about the main verbs you identified in activity 2.

- [ ] They are in the infinitive ("to" + verb).
- [ ] They are in the imperative (verb).
- [ ] In "Don't wait until you're thirsty [...].", the main verb is in the negative form.
- [ ] In "Drink plenty of water [...].", the verb is in the affirmative form.
- [ ] It is not necessary to use an auxiliary verb in negative imperative sentences.

4 Complete the recommendations using the verbs from the box. Follow the examples.

| not cheat | not forget | ~~not practice~~ | remember | take | warm up | ~~wear~~ |

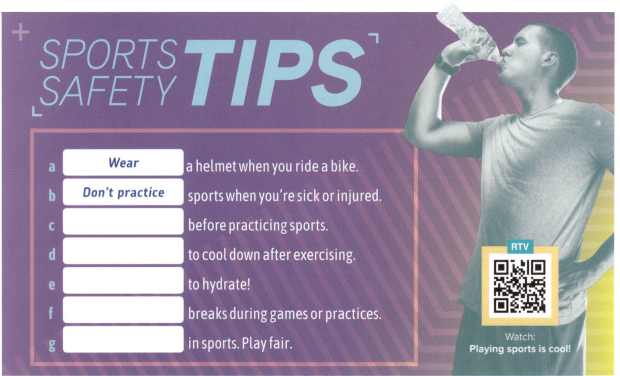

SPORTS SAFETY TIPS

a. **Wear** a helmet when you ride a bike.
b. **Don't practice** sports when you're sick or injured.
c. _____ before practicing sports.
d. _____ to cool down after exercising.
e. _____ to hydrate!
f. _____ breaks during games or practices.
g. _____ in sports. Play fair.

RTV
Watch: Playing sports is cool!

Sync Listening: Asking and answering questions about sports

Pre-listening

1 Look at the picture. What does it show? What are these people probably talking about?

Listening

2 Listen to Kristina, Michelle and McKenna interviewing students in an international school in South Korea. Match the students to their favorite sports.

a Macyn   ☐ baseball
b Sally   ☐ kickball
c Sarah   ☐ basketball
d KD Kim   ☐ soccer
e Bonne   ☐ tennis

> **Language clue**
>
> **interviewer** = the person who interviews
> **interviewee** = the person who is interviewed

3 Listen to the interviews again and write *T* (true) or *F* (false).

a ☐ There is an introduction in the beginning of the audio.
b ☐ The interviewees talk about the sports they don't like.
c ☐ All the interviewers introduce themselves.
d ☐ All the interviewers say the name of the person they are going to interview.
e ☐ Only two interviewers thank the person they talked to.

Post-listening

4 Which of the five interviewees (Macyn, Sally, Sarah, KD Kim or Bonne) are you most like? Consider their favorite sports.

L3

Sync Speaking: A survey on sports

Pre-speaking

1 What is a survey? Use the words from the box to complete a simplified definition.

| conduct | group (2x) | investigate | method | preferences |

In simple terms, a survey is a _____ of collecting information from a sample _____ of people. Usually, people _____ a survey in order to generalize the results to a larger _____ of people. A survey can be used to _____, for example, opinions, _____, behaviors etc. of a certain group.

Based on <https://www.qualtrics.com/experience-management/research/survey-basics/>. Accessed on April 22, 2019.

2 Let's prepare a survey on sports habits. Follow the instructions.
  a Review the language related to sports presented in this chapter.
  b Write some questions about sports habits and preferences. Use the "Useful language" box to help you.
  c Get together in small groups. Decide which questions your group is going to use in the survey.
  d Decide how many students each member of your group is going to interview.
  e Get ready to answer questions from members of the other groups as well.

Useful language

Questions
What is your favorite sport?
Where do you play/practice/do it?
When do you play/practice/do it?
Why do you like it?

Answers
My favorite sport is (volleyball).
I play/practice/do it (at the recreational club).
I play/practice/do it (on Mondays and Wednesdays).
I like it because (it's fun).

Speaking

3 Conduct the survey. Go around the classroom interviewing your classmates. Write down their answers in order to present the results later.

Post-speaking

4 Think about the survey your group has conducted. Which part of it did you like most to be involved in? Check the best options for you.

☐ preparing the questions
☐ asking the questions
☐ answering the questions
☐ putting the information together
☐ preparing the presentation
☐ making the presentation

What: a poster
To whom: other students; the school community
Media: paper; digital
Objective: motivate people to practice sports and maintain a healthy lifestyle

1. Review all the information related to posters in this chapter.
2. Consider the elements that make up a poster. Make a list.
3. Find pictures that best express the idea you want to communicate.
4. Write the text of your poster. Use clear and grammatically adequate sentences.
5. Think about the size and the position of the pictures.
6. Think about the size and the colors of the poster.
7. Share your first draft with your classmates and teacher. Listen to their comments.
8. Revise and make adjustments to your text based on the feedback you have received.
9. Put up your poster in an appropriate place at school.
10. Publish your text on the **Students for PEACE Social Media** <www.studentsforpeace.com.br>, using the tag **myposter** or others chosen by the students.

8 This is me

Goals
- Deliver a presentation about your free-time activities.
- Learn how to use verb patterns with "hate", "like" and "love" + "to".
- Raise awareness of the importance of leisure time in our lives.
- Review the use of the present continuous.
- Review the use of the present simple.
- Understand and write texts for the "About me" section of blogs.
- Understand different people talking about their leisure activities.

Spark

1 Match the pictures to their descriptions. Write the corresponding numbers.

- [ ] A boy painting, apparently as a volunteer worker.
- [ ] A group of people watching the sunset.
- [ ] A girl making collage with paper and scissors.
- [ ] A teenager in a wheelchair practicing at a skate park.
- [ ] A girl reading a book.
- [ ] A boy posing underwater.
- [ ] A family playing ball together in a field.
- [ ] Someone playing a video game.

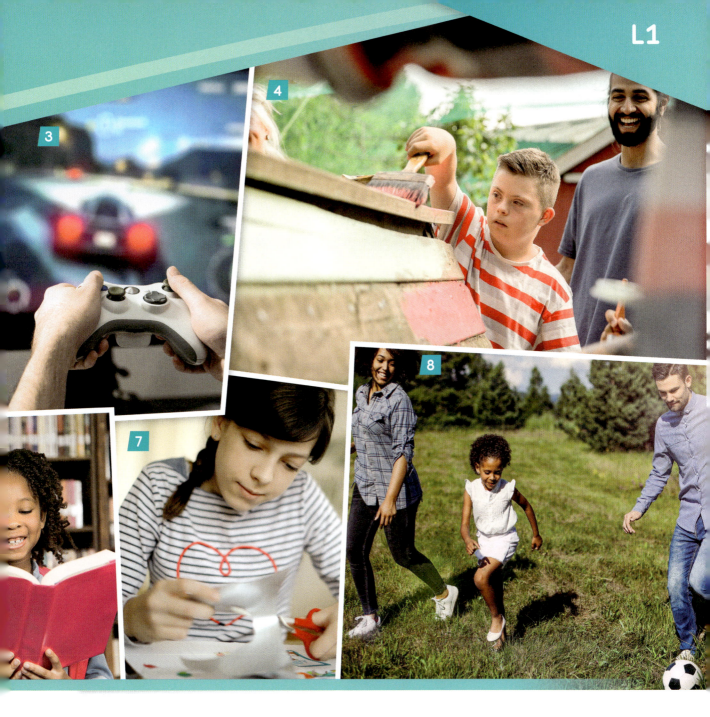

2 What do all the pictures have in common? Check the appropriate option.

- [ ] They all show people doing outdoor activities.
- [ ] They all show people doing indoor activities.
- [ ] They all show people doing things in their free time.
- [ ] They all include people with some type of disability.

Language clue

indoor = done in the interior of a building
outdoor = done outside a building, at open air

3 Answer the questions.

a Which picture is most connected to what you do in your free time?
b Which free-time activities do you like best?

L1

Explore "About me" blog section

Pre-reading

1 Take a look at texts 1 and 2. Then do the activities.

a Check the appropriate option for each question.

I In what type of blog can these texts most commonly appear?
- [ ] In a travel blog.
- [ ] In a personal blog.
- [ ] In a fashion blog.

II What pieces of information can we usually find in this type of blog?
- [ ] Information about age, marital status, height, weight.
- [ ] Home address, telephone number, e-mail.
- [ ] Name, personal traits, habits, preferences.

III Why do people usually decide to write about themselves in this type of blog?
- [ ] To receive criticism and comments from other people.
- [ ] To create empathy with the readers.
- [ ] To sell the blog space for sponsors and businesses.

b Who usually writes personal blogs? Who is their intended audience? Talk to your classmates.

Text 1

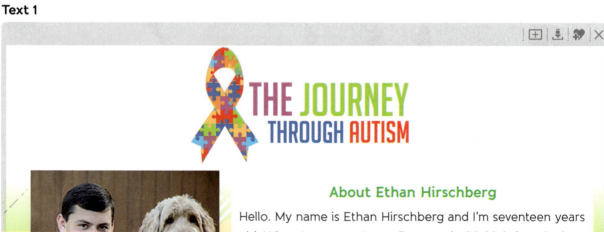

About Ethan Hirschberg

Hello. My name is Ethan Hirschberg and I'm seventeen years old. When I was two, I was diagnosed with high functioning autism. [...] I live with my parents, little brother, and two Goldendoodles! Because of my special needs, my brother and I fight more than other siblings, but we make it work. My family still stays strong. They are my rock and I love them to the moon and back.

I absolutely love to write (especially blogging). Besides writing and school, I like to hang out with family and friends, practice martial arts, cook, and run my own business. [...]

Ethan Hirschberg, personal autism blogger

Available at <https://www.thejourneythroughautism.com/about-me>. Accessed on January 25, 2019.

Text 2

ABOUT EL AND JAE

Hello and welcome to Eljae, a glasses-powered blog brought to you by the letters El and Jae. It's the world's first mother and daughter blog*.

*Disclaimer – it might not be

El is also known as Lia, a 13-year-old girl living by the seaside in the UK. El likes reading, films, history, and more reading.

Jae is Joanne, who is Lia's mum and is really ancient. Jae likes films (any films), writing and baking. Jae [...] is still finding out about teenagers. [...]

We both wear glasses. We both live in the same house. Other than that we are very different. El has long hair for a start.

OTHER PEOPLE YOU MAY MEET:

Eye is El's little brother.
ElDad is El's dad.
Dennis the cat is a cat. He's quite grumpy and slightly evil but still cute.
[...]

Available at <https://eljae.com/about/>. Accessed on January 25, 2019.

Reading

2 Read the two texts. Then answer the questions by writing the corresponding names of people mentioned in the texts.

a Who is 13 years old? _____

b Who is 17 years old? _____

c Who is not a teenager? _____

d Who has two dogs? _____

e Who has a cat? _____

f Who wears glasses? _____

g Who has a daughter? _____

h Who has a brother? _____

Going further

The word "blog" is short for "weblog", a combination of "web" and "log". The word "log" means a record of facts or daily events. Blogs have emerged in the final years of the 20th century as webpages that contain narratives of everyday life or personal reflections on a specific theme. With the popularization of blogs, their objectives and formats have diversified. As video sharing websites have also popularized, neologisms such as "vlog" ("video" + "log") were also created. A "vlog" is a blog whose content is exclusively produced on video.

L1

3 Read texts 1 and 2 again and check if the statements are *T* (true) or *F* (false). Correct the false ones.

a ☐ Ethan likes to hang out with his friends only.
_____

b ☐ Ethan loves to write all kinds of things equally.
_____

c ☐ Both El and Jae like to watch films.
_____

d ☐ El has short hair.
_____

e ☐ Ethan practices martial arts.
_____

f ☐ El doesn't like to read very much.
_____

4 Read these sentences taken from the texts and check the appropriate options.

a The sentence "[...] I love them to the moon and back." refers to…

☐ how much Ethan likes his hobbies.   ☐ how much Ethan loves his family.
☐ how much Ethan loves his followers.

b The sentence "Jae [...] is still finding out about teenagers." means that…

☐ she doesn't know everything about teenagers.
☐ she is a teenager.
☐ she knows everything about teenagers.

Post-reading

5 Would you follow any of the bloggers in texts 1 and 2? If so, who and why? Talk to a partner and present your reasons. You can use some of the ideas below.

I would follow…

Ethan   El and Jae

because…

… his story is inspiring.   … I like their writing style.

… I'd like to understand what autism is.   … their posts are probably interesting.

… his posts are probably interesting.   … I like the idea of a mother and daughter blog.

… I like people who like dogs.   … I like the idea of a glasses-powered blog.

L2

Toolbox — Present simple and present continuous (review), verb pattern ("hate", "like", "love" + "to")

1 Read these five comic strips. Then tell a partner which one you liked best and why.

Text 1

Text 2

Text 3

Text 4

Text 5

2 Now do the following activities based on some examples from the texts in activity 1.

a Write "CA" (continuous action) for sentences that express an action happening at the moment of speaking and "RA" (routine action) for sentences that express a routine (or habitual) action.

☐ "[Are you] getting some rest?" ☐ "I'm doing nothing."
☐ "But I don't like to talk about them." ☐ "I love to smear it on my body."
☐ "I hate Mondays."

b Match the columns to complete the rules. Draw lines to connect the bullets. The first one is done for you.

I To express actions that are happening at the moment of speaking (affirmative), we use…

II To express routine or habitual actions (affirmative), we use…

III The pattern for questions about actions that are happening at the moment of speaking is…

IV The pattern for questions about habitual or routine actions is…

- (wh- word) + do/does + subject + main verb.
- the present simple (subject + main verb, with the necessary changes for 3rd person singular).
- the present continuous (subject + verb to be + main verb + -ing).
- (wh- word) + verb to be + subject + main verb + -ing.

3 Imagine you are texting with your friends and they write the messages below. How would you react? Write the letter corresponding to the emoji you would use.

a 😍 love   b 😃 like   c 🙁 don't like   d 😠 hate

- I ☐ I'm watching a horror movie.
- II ☐ My dad is making lasagna for dinner.
- III ☐ We're watching a soccer game.
- IV ☐ My dog is here playing with me.
- V ☐ My cousins are here listening to reggaeton.

4 Read the comic strips in activity 1 again and follow the instructions.

a Find examples of sentences with the verb "hate". Write them down.

_____

b Find an example of sentence with the verb "like". Write it down.

_____

c Find examples of sentences with the verb "love". Write them down.

_____

5 Look at the examples you identified in activity 4 and complete these sentences with the appropriate options.

a The verbs "hate", "like" and "love" can be followed by...

☐ nouns only.
☐ nouns or verbs.
☐ verbs only.

b When the verbs "hate", "like" and "love" are followed by other verbs...

☐ we use "to" after these three verbs.
☐ we use the verbs only.
☐ we use "to" before these three verbs.

> **Language clue**
> leisure = activities people do when they are not working or studying

6 Write about yourself. Then share your answers with a partner.

a In my free time I hate to _____.

b In my spare time I like to _____.

c In my leisure time I love to _____.

L2

Building blocks — Free-time activities

1 How well can you name free-time activities in English? Test yourself by matching the pictures to what they represent. Then check your answers with a partner.

- [ ] drawing
- [ ] flying a kite
- [ ] going out with friends
- [ ] listening to music
- [ ] playing an instrument
- [ ] playing video games
- [ ] playing/doing sports
- [ ] reading (books, comics etc.)
- [ ] singing
- [ ] texting friends
- [ ] visiting a museum/an art gallery
- [ ] watching TV (movies, cartoons etc.)

2 Classify the free-time activities from activity 1 according to the categories below. Write the names of the activities.

a Creative activities: _____

b Exercise: _____

c Social/Entertainment/Leisure: _____

d TV/Audio: _____

e Literary/Culture: _____

3 Talk to six classmates about free-time activities. Take notes on their answers.

> What do you like to do in your free time?

> I like to play the guitar, go out with friends and watch movies. What about you?

Useful language

When you don't know how to do something, you can use the question "Can you help me, please?" to ask your teacher to help you.

L3

Sync Listening: What do you do in your free time?

Pre-listening

1 When do people usually talk about their free-time activities?

2 What do these two pictures show? What do you think these people are talking about based on the topic of this section?

Listening

3 🎧 21 Listen to the audio extracts and answer the questions.

a What are the people talking about?

b What question was probably asked by the reporter?

☐ Do you like to play video games?

☐ What do you do in your free time?

4 🎧 21 Listen again and check the activities you hear.

☐ go to a museum   ☐ play video games   ☐ play the flute
☐ play badminton   ☐ swim in the river   ☐ dance
☐ talk to my friends   ☐ go on the computer   ☐ go swimming

Post-listening

5 Why do you think some people or institutions decide to interview people about their free-time activities? Use the ideas below in your answers, if you wish.

- to get information for a school project
- to make people think about the importance of leisure
- to launch new products
- to create content for their channel

L3

Sync Speaking: Presentation about free-time activities

Pre-speaking

1 Go back to the "Sync – Listening" section and do these activities.

a Consider the context of the audio. Check other questions that were probably asked by the reporter besides "What do you do in your free time?".

- [ ] Are you a good student?
- [ ] What's your name?
- [ ] Do you like lasagna?
- [ ] Do you live in a house?
- [ ] How old are you?
- [ ] Are you playing now?

b In what order were the three questions (including the one mentioned in the instructions to item "a") probably asked?

_____

c Now write answers to those three questions.

_____

d List some free-time activities that you don't like or perhaps that you hate.

_____

2 Consider the information you provided about yourself in activity 1. Choose what you want to include in your presentation. In your notebook, organize the order in which you will present it.

Speaking

3 Give your presentation so that your classmates can learn more about your likes and dislikes, and you can learn more about theirs.

> **Useful language**
> Hi, my name is…/I'm…
> I'm… years old.
> I like/love to… on the weekend/in my free time.
> I don't like to…
> I hate to…

Post-speaking

4 Talk about your experience.

a How can you improve the next presentation that you may make?

b What are some of the most popular free-time activities among your classmates?

Studio "About me" blog section

What: "About me" blog section containing free-time activities
To whom: other students; internet community
Media: paper; digital
Objective: share your interests and free-time activities

1. Review this chapter. Look for words you can use to write about what you like and what you don't like to do in your leisure.

2. Read the "About me" texts from this chapter and if possible from the internet as well. Write down words, expressions or phrases bloggers commonly use in this type of text.

3. Decide what pieces of information you want to include in your text.

4. Organize them into topics. Write sentences about each piece of information.

5. Get together with some classmates. Share your text and read theirs. Make comments based on questions like:
   - Is the draft text clear?
   - Is all the important information there?
   - What can be added?
   - What can be taken out?

6. Think about your classmates' suggestions. Revise and edit your text individually based on their feedback.

7. Write your final text.

8. Share your work with your classmates. You can hang it on a bulletin board.

9. Publish your work on the **Students for PEACE Social Media** <www.studentsforpeace.com.br>, using the tag **thisisme** or others chosen by the students.

Peace talk

**Chapters 7 and 8
Sportsmanship**

1. Look at the pictures and answer the questions. Then share your answers with your classmates.

a. O que cada imagem mostra? Qual tema é comum a todas elas?

_____

_____

b. Em qual imagem é possível perceber que alguém abriu mão da sua posição na competição para ajudar outra pessoa? Como você avalia essa atitude?

_____

_____

c. Você já vivenciou alguma situação parecida com essas? Se sim, compartilhe.

_____

_____

2 Match each picture from activity 1 to its corresponding caption.

a ☐ Japanese football player Azusa Iwashimizu (left) comforts French player Camille Abily at the end of their semi-final Japan versus France event at Wembley Stadium, on the occasion of the London 2012 Olympic Games, on August 6, 2012, in London, England

b ☐ Regis Laconi (left), from France, and Troy Corser, from Australia, greet each other during an interruption due to rain at the 2005 Superbike World Championship, in Australia

c ☐ Adefolarin Durosinmi, of Sisaket Football Club (right), showing sportsmanship during the Thai Premier League match at Sri Nakhon Lamduan Stadium, Sisaket, Thailand

d ☐ A runner helps another runner reach the finish line during the 118th edition of the Boston Marathon, on April 21, 2014, in Boston, Massachusetts, United States

3 Talk about the situations presented in activities 1 and 2 with a partner.

a O que você sentiu ao ver e ler sobre essas histórias?

b Que sentimentos provavelmente levaram essas pessoas a colaborar com os/as oponentes?

c Qual deve ser, provavelmente, a visão dessas pessoas sobre os esportes e as competições? Por quê?

d Como você teria agido em cada situação? Por quê?

e Você já vivenciou alguma experiência em que decidiu parar o que estava fazendo para auxiliar alguém? Se sim, o que aconteceu e por que agiu assim?

4 Make a presentation to show examples of sportsmanship. Follow the instructions.

a Em grupos, listem atitudes que demonstrem o que é ter e o que é não ter espírito esportivo.

b Listem situações em que essas atitudes poderiam ocorrer, como as que foram apresentadas nesta seção.

c Escolham uma das atitudes listadas. Preparem o roteiro de uma cena em que não haja espírito esportivo, uma em que, na mesma situação, haja espírito esportivo e, por fim, uma cena de conclusão com uma mensagem final. Por exemplo:

Cena 1: Duas pessoas jogando tênis de mesa. Uma erra a jogada, atira a raquete para longe e abandona o jogo no meio, mal-humorada. **Cena 2:** Duas pessoas jogando tênis de mesa. Uma delas erra a jogada e cumprimenta o/a oponente pela bela jogada que este/esta fez. **Cena 3:** Narração: "*Good players respect and value their opponents.*".

d Decidam quem fará cada papel e como realizarão a apresentação.

Self-assessment

Chapter 1 – English everywhere

Can you understand the organization of a bilingual dictionary entry?

Can you understand and use the genitive case ('s)?

Can you say the alphabet in English?

Can you spell words in English?

Chapter 2 – Identities

Can you talk about yourself?

Can you understand texts about other people?

Can you introduce yourself?

Can you write a scrapbook with important information about yourself?

Chapter 3 – Family

Can you understand and use vocabulary about family members?

Can you read, understand and create a comic strip?

Can you understand and use personal pronouns?

Can you understand and use possessive adjectives?

Chapter 4 – School life

Can you understand when people write or speak about their school routines?

Can you use the present simple to talk about school routines?

Can you introduce yourself and talk about your school routines?

Can you organize a timetable and describe it?

Chapter 5 – Connected

Can you identify a meme?

Can you describe the characteristics of a meme?

Can you talk about your household chores?

Are you able to tell who does household chores in your house?

Chapter 6 – Networking

Can you understand a text message?

Can you write a text message describing what you are doing?

Can you choose between formal and informal language in a text message?

Can you understand the meaning of emojis in a text message?

Chapter 7 – Sports

Can you identify the main elements of a poster?

Can you name some sports?

Can you use the imperative to give recommendations?

Can you prepare a simple survey?

Chapter 8 – This is me

Can you understand the essential information in an "About me" section of a blog?

Can you understand written and oral texts in which people express their likes and dislikes?

Can you talk and write about your free-time activities?

Can you write a text for an "About me" section of a blog?

Workbook

Name: _____ Class: _____ Date: _____

Chapter 1 English everywhere

1 Read the text and write *T* (true) or *F* (false).

> house – *noun*
> \hauṡ\
> *plural* houses \ˈhau̇-zəz also -səz\
> 1: a building that serves as living quarters for one or more families;
> 2: a shelter or refuge of a wild animal;
> 3: a family, including ancestors and descendants: the *house* of Tudor.
>
> house – *verb*
> \hau̇z\
> 1: to give shelter, protection;
> 2: to store in a building: We *house* our boat in the garage.
>
> Adapted from <https://www.merriam-webster.com/dictionary/house>.
> Accessed on March 7, 2019.

a ☐ The text is part of a book about houses.
b ☐ The text is a dictionary entry.
c ☐ The word "house" functions as a verb and a noun.
d ☐ The text helps with the pronunciation of the word.
e ☐ The text gives three examples.

2 Read the sentences taken from the examples of four online dictionary entries. Find in each sentence one or more words we use in Brazilian contexts as well. Circle them.

a "We skate at the park."
b "The download will take about three minutes."
c "He learned to surf when he was living in California."
d "They served hot dogs and hamburgers."

Source: <https://www.merriam-webster.com/dictionary/>. Accessed on March 20, 2019.

3 Connect to the word in the center the ones that relate to it more commonly.

elephant — hamburger — pizza — **delivery** — dog — school — motorcycle — boy — house

113

4. English is everywhere. Look at this picture taken in Hong Kong. Find words in English and write them down.

5. Look at the pictures and write about them, as in the examples.

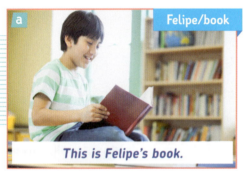

a. Felipe/book

This is Felipe's book.

b. Joana/bicycle

c. Pietra and Paulo/father

d. Keila/Nora/dogs

These are

e. Julia/cats

Workbook

Name: _____ Class: _____ Date: _____

Chapter 2 Identities

1 Look at the pictures and match them to the appropriate captions.

☐ Kevin Goodman on his new radio program, Teen Talk

☐ Fourteen-year-old Yula Koch scores her first goal

☐ Brazilian paralympic champion Daniel Dias in London

☐ Kaiko Hale and his small family at home in Hawaii

2 Complete the sentences with the appropriate form of the verb to be.

My name _____ Tasha Sesay. I _____ from Nsukka.
I _____ Nigerian. I _____ the number one biker in my school.

This _____ Ella Marija Lani Yelich-O'Connor. Her stage name _____ Lorde. She _____ a singer from New Zealand.

We _____ Wenwen Jiang and Tingting Jiang. We _____ synchronized swimmers. We _____ from China.

115

3 Solve the math equations and write the numbers in full. Follow the example.

a 12 × 6 = __72__

___twelve___ times ___six___ equals ___seventy-two___

b 81 ÷ 9 = _____

_____ divided by _____ equals _____

c 93 − 35 = _____

_____ minus _____ equals _____

4 Read this scrapbook page and write *T* (true) or *F* (false).

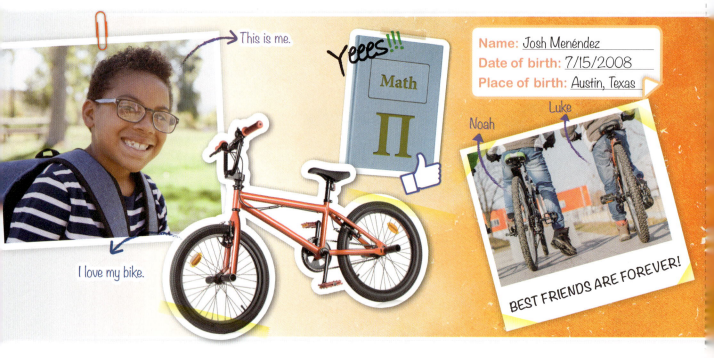

a ☐ Josh's birthday is in August.
b ☐ Luke is one of his best friends.
c ☐ His favorite sport is bike riding.
d ☐ Josh's hometown is in Texas.
e ☐ His last name is Noah.
f ☐ Math isn't one of his favorite subjects.

5 Complete this paragraph about Josh using information from the scrapbook page above.

This is _____. His birthday is on _____.

His hometown is _____. _____ is bike riding.

_____ are Noah and Luke.

6 Now write about yourself. Use the paragraph in activity 5 as an example.

_____
_____

Workbook

Name: _____ Class: _____ Date: _____

Chapter 3 Family

1 Look at this family tree. Then write *T* (true) or *F* (false).

a ☐ Nicole is Dylan's mother.
b ☐ Dylan is Isabella's brother.
c ☐ Amelia is Ava's aunt.
d ☐ Ava is Zach's sister.
e ☐ Linda is Jacob's grandmother.
f ☐ Anthony is Dylan's father.

2 Look at the family tree in activity 1 and answer these questions.

a Who is Charlotte's daughter?
_____

b Who is Lucca's grandmother?
_____

c Who is Amelia's father-in-law?
_____

d Who are Zoey's parents?
_____

e Who are Jacob's sisters?
_____

f Who are Andrew's grandsons?
_____

3. Read the blog page and complete the paragraphs with the appropriate possessive adjectives.

Students for Peace — Abasi's blog

about me | pictures | more info

Hello, I'm Abasi and I'm a student. _____ friends and I are from Kilgoris, Kenya. We're Maasai. _____ school is very special, and _____ teachers are friendly. We use e-books to read in English. _____ tablet is my treasure. _____ stories are very interesting and funny. All _____ friends love _____ tablets as well. Mr. Mbogo is _____ English teacher. He likes _____ tablet too.

How about you? Do you like _____ school?

4. Read Greta Thunberg's profile and answer the questions. For negative answers, add the appropriate information.

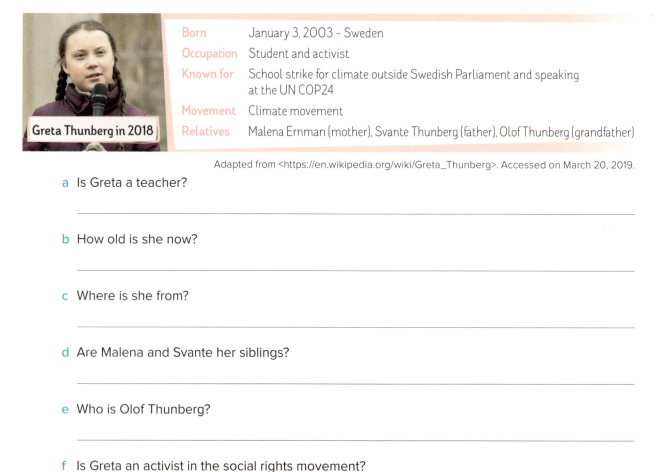

Born	January 3, 2003 – Sweden
Occupation	Student and activist
Known for	School strike for climate outside Swedish Parliament and speaking at the UN COP24
Movement	Climate movement
Relatives	Malena Ernman (mother), Svante Thunberg (father), Olof Thunberg (grandfather)

Greta Thunberg in 2018

Adapted from <https://en.wikipedia.org/wiki/Greta_Thunberg>. Accessed on March 20, 2019.

a Is Greta a teacher?

b How old is she now?

c Where is she from?

d Are Malena and Svante her siblings?

e Who is Olof Thunberg?

f Is Greta an activist in the social rights movement?

Workbook

Name: _____ Class: _____ Date: _____

Chapter 4 — School life

1 Read Laureen's school timetable and check the appropriate statements.

Period	Time	MONDAY	TUESDAY	WEDNESDAY	THURSDAY	FRIDAY
1st	9:00	English	English	Math	Math	Math
2nd	9:40	English	English	Math	Math	Math
	10:20	Recess	Recess	Recess	Recess	Recess
3rd	10:40	Math	Physical Education	English	English	English
4th	11:20	Math	Geography	English	English	French
	12:00	Lunch	Lunch	Lunch	Lunch	Lunch
	12:45	Silent reading	Silent reading	Silent reading	Silent reading	Silent reading
5th	12:55	French	Science	Music	Physical Education	Geography
6th	1:35	Science	French	CI*	CI*	Science
7th	2:15	Library	Math	CI*	CI*	Art

* Curriculum Integration   Based on <https://wells6.weebly.com/class-schedule.html>. Accessed on March 10, 2019.

a ☐ Laureen has three Science classes a week.
b ☐ She has Physical Education on Tuesdays and Fridays.
c ☐ Math is her last class on Tuesdays.
d ☐ Laureen has one Music class a week.
e ☐ She doesn't have French classes.

2 Read Laureen's school timetable again and answer the questions.

a What time does Laureen have lunch every day?
_____

b What time does Laureen have recess every day?
_____

c What is her last class on Fridays?
_____

d When does Laureen go to the library?
_____

3 Compare Laureen's school timetable to yours. Identify two differences and two similarities and write them.

Differences: _____
Similarities: _____

119

4 Complete the sentences with "in", "on", "at", "from" or "to".

a His Math class starts _____ 3 o'clock.

b My sister has lunch _____ 1:45 p.m. _____ 2:45 p.m. every day.

c Their birthday is _____ November.

d I have guitar lessons _____ Mondays and Wednesdays.

5 Read Frank's summer schedule and write *T* (true) or *F* (false).

SUMMER SCHEDULE

Monday	Tuesday	Wednesday	Thursday	Friday	Saturday
family movie night	take a trip	science experiment	park	friend	swim

Adapted from <http://defeatingbusy.com/make-moms-kids-happy-with-a-summer-schedule/>. Accessed on March 10, 2019.

a ☐ Frank rides his bicycle on Tuesdays.

b ☐ Saturday is the day when he goes swimming.

c ☐ He has a family program on Mondays.

d ☐ He goes to school on Tuesdays.

6 Answer questions a-b based on activity 5. Then answer questions c-d about yourself.

a What does Frank do on Tuesdays?
_____

b Where do you think Frank goes on Sundays?
_____

c What about you? What do you do when you are on vacation?
_____

d What time do you go to bed on your ideal summer vacation?
_____

Workbook

Name: _____ Class: _____ Date: _____

Chapter 5 Connected

1 Read Cody and Lynn's weekly schedule and write *T* (true) or *F* (false).

	SUN	MON	TUE	WED	THU	FRI	SAT
morning	floor - C/L cat - L	bed - C/L cat - L	bed - C/L cat - L	bed - C/L cat - L	bed - C/L cat - L	bed - C/L cat - L	bed - C/L cat - L
afternoon	table - C						table - L
evening	dog - L	trash - C dog - C	trash - L dog - C	trash - C dog - C	trash - L dog - C	trash - C dog - C	dog - L

C = Cody; L = Lynn

a ☐ Lynn walks the dog only on Saturdays.

b ☐ Cody never feeds the cat.

c ☐ Cody and Lynn don't have any household chores in the afternoon on weekdays.

d ☐ They sweep the floor once a week.

2 Complete the sentences with "usually", "sometimes" or "never" according to the schedule in activity 1.

a Lynn _____ does the laundry.

b Cody and Lynn _____ make their beds.

c Cody _____ clears or sets the table.

3 Now answer the questions based on the schedule in activity 1.

a When does Cody walk the dog?
_____

b What does Lynn do on Saturday afternoon?
_____

c Who takes out the trash on Thursdays?
_____

4 Complete the sentences with the appropriate form of the verbs in parentheses.

a My brother _____ (do) the laundry on Saturday morning.

b A: _____ Mario _____ (do) the dishes?

B: Yes, he _____ (do) the dishes.

c A: Who _____ (feed) the cat in your home?

B: My sister and I. We _____ (feed) our cat every day.

d Laura _____ (sweep) the floor every morning.

5 Read the cartoon. Then circle the appropriate options.

PLAN A
☐ do Math exercises
☐ do a Science experiment
☐ do my History homework
☐ clean my bedroom
☐ wash the dog

PLAN B
☐ play video games all day

I ALWAYS HAVE A PLAN B!

a The boy has **two/three** household chores to do.

b He **thinks/doesn't think** about the consequences of his plan B.

c The boy **likes/doesn't like** his plan B.

d The boy probably **gets/doesn't get** very good grades in Math.

e Cleaning the bedroom **is/isn't** part of the boy's plan B.

6 Think about your week. Complete the sentences with the days of the week and the adverbs "always", "usually", "sometimes" or "never".

a On _____ I _____ wash the dishes.

b On _____ I _____ do my homework.

c On _____ I _____ clean my bedroom.

d On _____ I _____ study.

e On _____ I _____ watch TV or play video games.

Workbook

Name: _____ Class: _____ Date: _____

Chapter 6 Networking

1 Read the text. Then do the activities.

a According to the text...

☐ Doug and Luke are in the same place.

☐ At first, Doug doesn't believe what Luke tells him.

☐ Luke's brother has a dog.

☐ We don't know why Doug is texting Luke.

☐ Since the beginning, Henry knows that Luke is painting a portrait of a dog.

b Write *T* (true) or *F* (false).

☐ When Doug says "U WHAT?", he is surprised.

☐ Luke probably likes his Art classes.

☐ In Doug's opinion, painting a portrait of a dog is a bad idea.

☐ The sentence "U arent doin that, dude" also expresses Doug's surprise.

c Rewrite these sentences in full.

I what u doing

II whats wrong w/ paintin a portrait of a dog?

_____   _____

d Which picture shows that Doug is thinking about Luke's actions?

☐   ☐

2 What are these people doing?

a What's Layla doing?

_____

b What's her father doing?

_____

c What's her brother doing?

_____

3 What are these people's nationalities?

Ed Sheeran is from England.

He's _____.

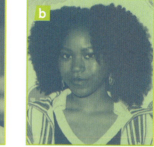

Riele Downs is from Canada.

She's _____.

Cristiano Ronaldo is from Portugal.

He's _____.

Zaz is from France.

She's _____.

Workbook

Name: _____ Class: _____ Date: _____

Chapter 7 Sports

1 Read this poster and check the appropriate options.

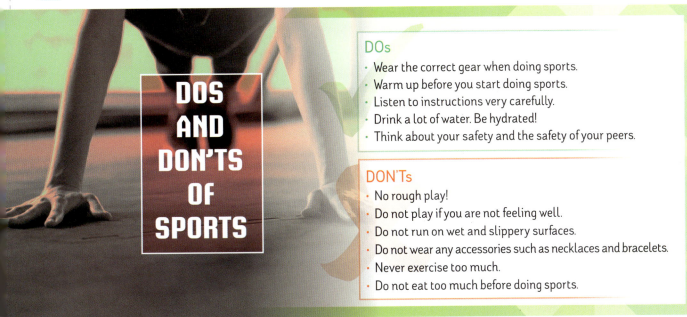

DOs
- Wear the correct gear when doing sports.
- Warm up before you start doing sports.
- Listen to instructions very carefully.
- Drink a lot of water. Be hydrated!
- Think about your safety and the safety of your peers.

DON'Ts
- No rough play!
- Do not play if you are not feeling well.
- Do not run on wet and slippery surfaces.
- Do not wear any accessories such as necklaces and bracelets.
- Never exercise too much.
- Do not eat too much before doing sports.

Adapted from <https://pt.slideshare.net/kokliyingXD/green-house-sports-dos-and-donts>. Accessed on March 29, 2019.

a Who is this poster for?
- [ ] For people that are familiar with the practice of sports.
- [ ] For people that do not practice sports regularly.

b Another word for "rough" is...
- [ ] "nice".
- [ ] "violent".

c Why is it important to listen to instructions very carefully?
- [ ] To know what you can do and what you cannot do.
- [ ] To be the champion.

d What is the objective of this poster?
- [ ] To give orders.
- [ ] To make recommendations.

2 Read the sentences and write *T* (true) or *F* (false) according to the poster in activity 1.
- [ ] If you run on a wet floor, you can slip and fall.
- [ ] If you wear a necklace, you have more chances of winning the game.
- [ ] It is not necessary to warm up before playing a game.
- [ ] It is very important to drink water when you practice a sport.

3. Check the suitable gear for cycling.

4. Look at the pictures and label the sports.

5. What parts of the body do we use most when we do these sports? Follow the example and complete.

   a When we surf, we use our *legs and arms* _____.

   b When we play soccer, we use our _____.

   c When we play tennis, we use our _____.

   d When we do gymnastics, we use our _____.

   e When we ride a bicycle, we use our _____.

Chapter 8 This is me

1 Read the text and check the appropriate options.

a Natori's first language...
- [ ] is probably English.
- [ ] is probably not English.

b In the morning, Natori...
- [ ] goes to school.
- [ ] practices running.

c Masii is...
- [ ] a small place in Kenya.
- [ ] very far from Nairobi.

2 Read the sentences and write *T* (true) or *F* (false) according to the text in activity **1**.

a [ ] Natori knows what he wants to be.
b [ ] Natori likes to fly.
c [ ] Tuwile is a runner.
d [ ] Natori has a cousin that doesn't like to run.

3 Now answer the questions about the text in activity 1.

a What is the meaning of the boy's name?
___

b What are the three things Natori mentions he likes?
___

c What sentence in the text may allow us to say that Masii is not a big city?
___

4 Complete the sentences with the appropriate form of the verbs in parentheses.

a
I'm Nathan and I usually ___ (swim), but I ___ (not swim) now. I ___ (cycle).

b
Natalie ___ (play) tennis at the moment, but in the morning she always ___ (run).

c

Marcos and Felipe ___ (play) football now. They ___ (play) football after school every day.

d

Look! Manoela ___ (talk) to Jeremy in the schoolyard. They're good friends and they always ___ (talk) during recess.

5 What do you like to do in your free time? Is there anything you don't like to do?
___
___

Language reference

Chapter 1 — Genitive case ('s)

O *genitive case* (*'s*) é usado para indicar uma relação de posse, ou seja, que algo pertence ou está relacionado a alguém. Observe como ele é geralmente formado em inglês:

Possuidor	Apóstrofo + s (regra geral)	Exemplos
substantivo singular	's	Maria**'s** book
substantivo plural terminado em *s*	'	my friend**s'** books
substantivo plural irregular	's	the children**'s** books
nome próprio terminado em *s*	's (ou apenas ')	Marcos**'s** book / Ms. Jones**'** book

(Possuidor + Apóstrofo + s)

Quando há mais de um possuidor:

- acrescenta-se *'s* apenas ao último se eles possuem juntos o mesmo elemento:
  This is **David** and **Mike's** bedroom.

- acrescenta-se *'s* a todos os possuidores se cada um possui seu próprio elemento:
  These are **Ava's** and **Sophia's** bedrooms.

Chapter 2 — Verb "to be"

O verbo *to be* ("ser" ou "estar") pode ser empregado, entre outras possibilidades, para identificar pessoas, coisas ou lugares e apontar suas características.

Parker **is** my sister.

Those books **are** very good.

This **is** the city where I live.

I **am** short and thin.

Observe como se conjuga o verbo *to be* no *present simple*:

Affirmative	Negative	Interrogative — Questions	Interrogative — Short answers
I am	I am not	Am I…?	Yes, you are. / No, you are not.
You are	You are not	Are you…?	Yes, I am. / No, I am not.
He is	He is not	Is he…?	Yes, he is. / No, he is not.
She is	She is not	Is she…?	Yes, she is. / No, she is not.
It is	It is not	Is it…?	Yes, it is. / No, it is not.
We are	We are not	Are we…?	Yes, we/you are. / No, we/you are not.
You are	You are not	Are you…?	Yes, we are. / No, we are not.
They are	They are not	Are they…?	Yes, they are. / No, they are not.

Nas formas afirmativa e negativa, é possível contrair o verbo *to be* usando o que chamamos de *contracted form*:

Affirmative	Negative
I'm	I'm not
You're	You're not / You aren't
He's	He's not / He isn't
She's	She's not / She isn't
It's	It's not / It isn't
We're	We're not / We aren't
You're	You're not / You aren't
They're	They're not / They aren't

Chapter 3 — Possessive adjectives

Na língua inglesa, a indicação de pertencimento a ou de relação com algo ou alguém pode ser feita com o uso do *genitive case*, como visto no Capítulo 1. Outra forma de fazê-lo é por meio dos pronomes possessivos adjetivos (*possessive adjectives*). Observe o quadro:

Subject pronouns	Possessive adjectives
I	**my** – meu, minha, meus, minhas
You	**your** – teu, tua, teus, tuas, seu, sua, seus, suas
He	**his** – dele, seu, sua, seus, suas
She	**her** – dela, seu, sua, seus, suas
It	**its** – dele, dela, seu, sua, seus, suas (neutro – refere-se a coisas em geral, ideias, lugares, animais e sentimentos)
We	**our** – nosso, nossa, nossos, nossas
You	**your** – vosso, vossa, vossos, vossas, seu, sua, seus, suas, de vocês
They	**their** – deles, delas, seu, sua, seus, suas

Os *possessive adjectives* sempre antecedem o substantivo ao qual se referem:

I know **her** father because he is a teacher at **our** school.

His cousin is Mexican.

Their twin sons are eleven years old.

Brazil is close to the equator and **its** climate is tropical.

Chapter 4 Present simple (affirmative)

Usa-se o *present simple* na afirmativa para se referir a:

- uma informação que é real no presente:
  My parents **live** in Toronto.

- uma ação que acontece sempre ou com alguma frequência:
  We **have** English classes on Mondays and Wednesdays.

- um fato ou uma verdade universal:
  Sound **travels** at a speed of around 1,230 kilometers per hour.

Se o verbo terminar em uma consoante seguida de *y*, como *to study*, retira-se o *y* e acrescenta-se *-ies*: stud**ies**. Se o verbo terminar em uma vogal seguida de *y*, como *to play*, acrescenta-se *-s*: play**s**.

Observe:

I	study	play
You	study	play
He	stud**ies**	play**s**
She	stud**ies**	play**s**
It	stud**ies**	play**s**
We	study	play
You	study	play
They	study	play

O verbo *to have* tem uma forma irregular na 3ª pessoa do singular:

I/You/We/They	have
He/She/It	has

Chapter 5 Present simple (affirmative, negative, interrogative)

Observe como se conjuga o verbo *to help* na afirmativa e na negativa do *present simple*:

Affirmative	Negative	
	Full form	Contracted form
I help	I do not help	I don't help
You help	You do not help	You don't help
He help**s**	He do**es** not help	He do**es**n't help
She help**s**	She do**es** not help	She do**es**n't help
It help**s**	It do**es** not help	It do**es**n't help
We help	We do not help	We don't help
You help	You do not help	You don't help
They help	They do not help	They don't help

Agora, observe a conjugação do verbo *to help* na interrogativa do *present simple*:

Interrogative	Short answers (affirmative)	Short answers (negative)
Do I help?	Yes, you do.	No, you don't.
Do you help?	Yes, I do.	No, I don't.
Do**es** he help?	Yes, he do**es**.	No, he do**es**n't.
Do**es** she help?	Yes, she do**es**.	No, she do**es**n't.
Do**es** it help?	Yes, it do**es**.	No, it do**es**n't.
Do we help?	Yes, we/you do.	No, we/you don't.
Do you help?	Yes, we do.	No, we don't.
Do they help?	Yes, they do.	No, they don't.

Chapter 6 Present continuous

O *present continuous* é usado para expressar o que está acontecendo no momento da fala ou escrita. O que caracteriza esse tempo verbal é o uso do verbo *to be* seguido do verbo principal com a terminação *-ing*. Observe:

Affirmative		
I	am	
You	are	
He		
She	is	walk**ing**.
It		
We		
You	are	
They		

Negative
She **is not** play**ing** soccer.

Interrogative
What **is** he do**ing**? **Are** they study**ing** English?
Who **are** you talk**ing** to? Where **are** you go**ing**?

Na maioria das vezes, basta acrescentar *-ing* à forma base do verbo principal: *talking*, *texting*. No entanto, em alguns casos, certas modificações são necessárias. Observe:

- Com verbos terminados em *e*, como *have*, *dance*, *live*, elimina-se essa letra e acrescenta-se *-ing*: *having*, *dancing*, *living*.
- Com verbos monossilábicos que terminam em consoante + vogal + consoante (verbos CVC), como *stop*, *get*, *swim*, dobra-se a última letra antes de acrescentar *-ing*: *stopping*, *getting*, *swimming*. Essa regra não se aplica a verbos com terminação em *x* ou *w*, como *fix* e *snow*: *fixing*, *snowing*.

Chapter 7 Imperative

O modo imperativo é empregado quando se deseja que alguém faça (ou não) alguma coisa. Pode ser encontrado em:

- comandos:

  Jump ten times and **stop**.

- pedidos, solicitações:

  Pass me the sugar, please.

- instruções:

  Press play to listen to your favorite song.

- conselhos:

  Go to the doctor if you are not feeling well.

- sugestões:

  If you want to laugh a lot, **watch** that new comedy. It's great!

Para formar o imperativo na negativa, usa-se o auxiliar *do* + *not*. Observe:

Do not forget to hydrate./**Don't forget** to hydrate.

Note que tanto no imperativo na afirmativa quanto na negativa o verbo principal é sempre usado no infinitivo.

Chapter 8 Verb pattern ("hate", "like", "love" + "to")

Os verbos *hate* (odiar, detestar), *like* (gostar, curtir) e *love* (amar, adorar) podem ser seguidos por outros verbos no infinitivo. Observe:

I **hate to wait** in line.

She **likes to read** paper magazines. She **doesn't like to read** online magazines.

We **don't like to play** volleyball.

They **love to cook**.

He **loves to paint**.

Interdisciplinary project
English: a global language

Presentation

Que tal conhecer mais sobre a dimensão intercultural da língua inglesa?

Procedures

Part I (Math and Geography)

Objective: map the countries where people speak English and in what contexts.
Resources: atlas (physical or digital), internet.

Instructions

a. Formem cinco grupos e sorteiem um dos continentes para cada grupo: África, América, Ásia, Europa e Oceania.

b. Pesquisem em livros ou na internet quais países do continente têm o inglês como língua materna ou língua oficial e em que contextos sociais ele é usado. Então, com o auxílio de um atlas, identifiquem esses países.

c. Descubram se a língua inglesa recebe algum nome diferente nesses países, por exemplo, *Hinglish, Taglish, Singapore English* etc. Compartilhem as informações com os demais grupos.

d. Façam um mapa do continente sorteado para o seu grupo indicando os países que usam o inglês e seu respectivo *status* (língua materna ou língua oficial).

e. Juntem os mapas de modo a formar um mapa-múndi com os cinco continentes.

f. Utilizem as informações do mapa-múndi para criar dois gráficos: um com a porcentagem de países em que o inglês está presente e outro com a proporção entre os diferentes *status* da língua. Os gráficos podem ser feitos por continente para facilitar a análise.

Analysis

Analisem o mapa e os gráficos e verifiquem em que continentes há maior presença do inglês como língua materna e em que continentes ele é mais frequente como língua oficial. O que esses dados indicam sobre a presença do inglês no mundo?

Reflections

Na opinião do grupo, por que o inglês (e não outro idioma) é a língua oficial nesses países? Registrem suas ideias para retomá-las na *Part II* do projeto.

Part II (History)

Objective: understand why English is present in a given country.
Resources: History books, internet.

Instructions

a. Reúnam-se com o mesmo grupo da *Part I* e escolham um dos países do continente sorteado para o seu grupo no qual a língua inglesa é usada como língua oficial.

b. Investiguem a história do país, buscando informações sobre como, quando e por que esse idioma chegou àquele país e se tornou oficial.

c. Listem as vantagens e desvantagens da adoção do inglês por esse país. Compartilhem as informações com outros grupos.

Analysis

Analisem a história do país e as vantagens e desvantagens de ele ter adotado o inglês como língua oficial. Anotem as conclusões.

Reflections

1. Que contribuições essa pesquisa trouxe para as discussões do item "Reflections" (*Part I*)? 2. O que é possível concluir sobre o efeito da expansão da língua inglesa no mundo? 3. Há algo em comum entre os dados apresentados e a presença do inglês no Brasil?

Part III (Math)

Objective: investigate the presence of English in your community.
Resources: data collected in field trips, internet.

Instructions

a. Em grupos e com a supervisão de um adulto, visitem diferentes ruas, procurando exemplos de uso do inglês. Anotem o tipo de local e o exemplo. Se possível, perguntem ao/à responsável pelos estabelecimentos, por exemplo, por que o nome do lugar, os itens do cardápio, a fachada do comércio etc. estão em inglês.

b. Organizem os dados em categorias: lojas (de roupas, sapatos etc.), beleza e saúde (salão, clínica, academia, clube etc.), alimentação e lazer (restaurante, cinema, parque etc.) e educação (escola, cursos etc.).

c. Compilem os dados em um gráfico que indique a porcentagem de uso do inglês por setor comercial.

d. Construam um questionário sobre o inglês no dia a dia dos/as amigos/as, familiares e pessoas da sua comunidade. Perguntem se essas pessoas ouvem/leem/falam/escrevem em inglês, com que frequência, com que finalidade e com quais culturas entram em contato por meio do inglês.

e. Realizem as entrevistas. Depois, usando as perguntas como categorias, compilem os dados em um gráfico representando o uso do inglês pelas pessoas entrevistadas.

Analysis

1. Com base nos exemplos de uso do inglês levantados no item "a", quais motivos justificam esse uso e quais deles são mais recorrentes? 2. Com base nos gráficos dos itens "c" e "e", o que vocês podem concluir sobre a presença do inglês no comércio e na vida das pessoas entrevistadas? 3. Em quais culturas o inglês está mais presente? 4. Vocês consideram que o uso do inglês pelo setor comercial busca um certo *status*? Em caso afirmativo, de onde vem esse *status*, em sua opinião?

Reflections

1. Vocês já tinham notado a presença do inglês na sua comunidade? 2. Na opinião de vocês, essa situação é igual em todas as partes do Brasil? Por quê? 3. Sua comunidade utiliza palavras em inglês quando há equivalentes em português? Se sim, quando e por quê? 4. Vocês acham que os filmes, jogos, séries etc. em inglês a que as pessoas são expostas influenciam o seu modo de pensar e agir? Se sim, de que forma?

Sharing knowledge

Que tal agora fazer uma exposição para a comunidade para apresentar o que vocês aprenderam nas diversas etapas do projeto?

Instructions

a. Se possível, peçam ajuda aos/às professores/professoras que acompanharam o projeto, apresentando as questões e respostas da seção "Reflections" de todas as etapas para que proponham alterações, quando necessárias, com o objetivo de levar essas questões para a comunidade.

b. Com base nas sugestões dos/as professores/professoras, preparem a versão final das questões para reflexão. Decidam como organizar e exibir os mapas e gráficos produzidos no projeto.

Presentation

Com a supervisão dos/as professores/professoras que auxiliaram na elaboração do projeto ao longo do ano e a presença de seu/sua professor/a de Língua Inglesa, apresentem para a comunidade os dados coletados e as análises feitas.

Assessment

Avaliem, com os/as professores/professoras que contribuíram para o projeto, os ganhos obtidos nas diversas etapas e na apresentação final. Avaliem, também, o que aprenderam sobre a importância da colaboração e do respeito para o sucesso do trabalho em grupo e para a superação das dificuldades que porventura tenham surgido.

Transcripts

Chapter 1

Track 4 – Page 16

Mary: Next is Carter Leonard and his favorite movie is *Star Wars*.

Bill: Here is your word, Carter. This word is "accommodate". Accommodate means "provide with lodgings": The hotel clerk explained that the hotel will accommodate guests who have pets if a two-hundred-dollar cleaning fee per night is paid. Accommodate.

Carter: Accommodate. A-C-C-O-M-O-D-A-T-E. Accommodate.

Bill: I'm sorry, there's two Ms. There are two Ms. Two Cs and two Ms. I'm sorry.

Track 6 – Page 17

A

Mary: Our first contestant is Victoria Smolen. She's 12 years old, from Onondaga Hill Middle School.

Bill: All right, Victoria, the first word this afternoon is *burrito*. Burrito: a flour *tortilla* rolled or folded around a filling, such as meat or beans or cheese, and usually baked: For lunch, Fred ordered a *burrito*, rice and refried beans. *Burrito*.

Victoria: Burrito. B-U-R-R-I-T-O.

Bill: Correct.

B

Mary: Next is Jonathan Hubbard and he would like to be a History teacher.

Bill: Jonathan, the word for you is *sevruga*. It's a light to dark gray caviar from a sturgeon of a genus found in the Caspian Sea that has very small roe. *Sevruga* has the strongest flavor of all sturgeon eggs. *Sevruga*.

Jonathan: Could I have the language of origin, please?

Bill: It is Russian.

Jonathan: Sevruga. Am I saying this correct?

Bill: You are! *Sevruga*.

Jonathan: Sevruga. S-E-V-R-U-G-A.

Bill: Correct.

Extracts from the audio available at <https://www.youtube.com/watch?v=9QAWJdItVkk>. Accessed on April 12, 2019.

Chapter 2

Track 8 – Page 29

Hi! My name is Nalinkarn. My nickname is Sydney. I'm 14 years old and I am an only child. [...] My favorite hobbies are playing sport[s], listening to music, reading novels, drawing and watching movies. And my favorite sport[s] are horse riding, swimming, sailing, badminton and basketball.

Extract from the audio available at <https://www.youtube.com/watch?v=AKH5kfqDq1k>. Accessed on April 12, 2019.

Track 9 – Page 29

1 Hi! I am from Turkey. I'm an only child. I like reading novels and watching movies.

2 Hi! I am from Brazil. I'm an only child. I like reading novels and watching movies.

3 Hi! I am from Ireland. I'm an only child. I like reading novels and watching movies.

4 Hi! I'm from Japan. I'm an only child. I like reading novels and watching movies.

5 Hi! I am from Australia. I'm an only child. I like reading novels and watching movies.

Chapter 3

Track 11 – Page 43

1 I'm blessed to have really, really nice parents and they are always looking out for me. That been said though, you do quarrel sometimes. I have a little brother who is about one years [*sic*] old—one year old—and my mom and I always argue because I have to watch him a lot and that's part of my job, as, you know, as a member of the family I do have to look after my siblings, so I always think I should not have to look after them for very long. I have a big sister who I can really talk to about a lot of stuff, especially when, you know, I just, I feel my inhibitions hold me back from talking to my mom and dad about it.

2 I do find it difficult to talk to my parents because they put a lot of pressure on me, saying I can tell them anything, but that just makes me feel like maybe they just wanna know and I am not so sure if I want to tell them about some of my problems.

3 When something is on my mind, I usually go to my friends about it, I don't really talk to my brother.

4 Every weekend, we have like a little family movie night or we just kick back and relax, watch a fun little movie, thus most of our arguments are over what movie we watch.

Extracts from the audio available at <https://www.youtube.com/watch?v=beuvyZfBFGQ>. Accessed on April 12, 2019.

This information was provided by KidsHealth®, one of the largest resources online for medically reviewed health information written for parents, kids and teens. For more articles like this, visit KidsHealth.org or TeensHealth.org. © 1995-2018. The Nemours Foundation/KidsHealth®. All rights reserved.

Track 12 — Page 43

Who am I? I'm Rose Rock... What does that mean? OK, you know, my claim to fame really is being Chris Rock's mom, but I'm so much more than that and I'm so over everybody calling me Chris Rock's mom. But anyway, I'm here today because we are doing a parenting conference and there is such a need now to reach out to parents to not only be better parents, but to be advocates for their children. Our children are in crisis mode. They're failing in school, the behavior outside of the school and whatnot and I'm old school and, basically, I believe that everything starts in the home.

Extract from the audio available at <https://www.youtube.com/watch?v=hnCsjwlYBPM>. Accessed on April 12, 2019.

Track 13 — Page 55

Hi, guys! My name is Honey and I'm 13 years old and today I am going to be showing you my homeschool routine. So, usually I start off the day by doing piano practice on the keyboard. [...] Another thing I do every day is I read some poetry [...] Another thing I do every day is I do some Latin out of this book and every day we just learn new words and it just explains what they mean and that's just another part of my homeschooling.

Track 14 — Page 55

So, every week, my mom will write out a checklist of all the books we have to read and it's up to us how many we want to do a day. And we usually try and do as many as possible [...]. So, the next book I have on my checklist is *Augustus Caesar's World* and this is my favorite book that I have to read out of all of them because it's just really interesting. [...] And then, after that, I have this book, *It Couldn't Just Happen*, which is really interesting. [...] This book is a science book and I really enjoy this book because Science is one of my favorite subjects.

Track 15 — Page 55

So, I used to go to secondary school, but I decided to be homeschooled as I preferred that a lot more because I was homeschooled before I went to secondary school and I definitely prefer it because it gives us a lot more freedom to get the work done in a shorter amount of time and to also have more holidays for the family and to spend more time together and also I like being homeschooled because I can focus on subjects I really like.

Extracts from the audio available at <https://www.youtube.com/watch?v=DhL2TEukczk>. Accessed on April 12, 2019.

Track 16 — Page 69

Hey, guys! A lot of people think "chores" and then they think "aaaw", because chores to some people aren't that fun, but they really don't have to be that bad. Like, there's a lot of chores that I actually like to do, like, organize, clean my bedroom, I actually enjoy doing and it's not that hard. And then it comes to the chores that I don't like, the laundry and dishes. Those aren't as fun, but I know that it helps out my family and I love having the feeling that, like, everything is clean now and it's all because of me. Then, I gonna go sit down and watch TV or something, but also it's a good thing if you get music while you're doing it because then, I don't know, I think it makes it seem more fun.

Extract from the audio available at <https://www.youtube.com/watch?v=t62MiqslfJQ>. Accessed on May 7, 2019.

Chapter 6

Track 17 — Page 81

Nicola: Hey, you're the new girl! You know it's the wrong uniform for this time of year, right?

Kelly: Yup, I've heard.

Nicola: I'm Nicola, but everyone calls me Nic.

Kelly: Hi, I'm Kelly.

Nicola: Wait, say it again.

Kelly: What? I'm Kelly.

Nicola: You're American! Oh, I love your accent! Say more things.

Kelly: What?

Nicola: Oh, just say more things so I can hear you talk.

Kelly: Apple pie, blizzard.

Nicola: Oh!

Kelly: Pillow fight, banana.

Nicola: You're funny!

Kelly: Thanks, this is my first day here.

Nicola: Oh, really? Where are you from? Why are you here? How long have you been here? What... Why are you at the gymnasium? Do you do gymnastics?

Kelly: Uh... I'm from Atlanta. I'm here with my mom for a year. She's a surgeon at the city hospital. I do... well, I did gymnastics.

Nicola: Oh, if you don't do gymnastics, why be here?

Kelly: I'm just sort of used to being in a gymnasium, it kind of feels like home. I don't really have any friends, so...

Nicola: Well, now you do.

Extract from a dialogue in the movie *Raising the Bar.* Director: Clay Glen. Australia: MarVista Entertainment, 2016. All media (93 min).

Chapter 7

Track 20 — Page 95

A

Kristina: Hi, I am Kristina! And Michelle, McKenna and I will interview people about what are [*sic*] their favorite sports. Let's get going. So here I am with Macyn. So, what is your favorite sport?

Macyn: My favorite sport is soccer because... well... it's really fun and my sister helped me with it.

Kristina: Thank you for interviewing [*sic*]. Bye.

B

Michelle: I'm with Sally. What's your favorite sport?

Sally: My favorite sport is basketball.

Michelle: Why is basketball your favorite sport?

Sally: I like basketball because it was my first team sport that I got to play. And then I feel very satisfied when I shoot a goal.

Michelle: Thank you.

C

Kristina: Hi... I'll interview Sarah about her favorite sport. So, what is your favorite sport?

Sarah: Kickball.

Kristina: Why do you like kickball?

Sarah: Because you kick the ball as hard as you can and then you run up to the first base, second base, third base, and then you go home, and you go like "safe".

Kristina: OK. Thank you, bye.

D

McKenna: Hi, KD. So, what's your favorite sport?

KD Kim: My favorite sport is tennis.

McKenna: Hmm... Why do you like tennis?

KD Kim: Because tennis is always filled with constant action.

McKenna: Hmm... Do you play tennis?

KD Kim: Yes. There is a tennis court behind the apartment where I live and I also have three tennis rackets.

McKenna: Cool. Thank you.

E

Michelle: Hi, I'm with Bonne. What's your favorite sport?

Bonne: Baseball.

Michelle: Why is baseball your favorite sport?

Bonne: Because my favorite things to do is [*sic*] catch, threw [*sic*] and hit.

Michelle: Why?

Bonne: It's fun.

Michelle: OK. Thank you.

Kristina: You guys like a lot of different kinds of sports. Thank you for interviewing who got interviewed. Bye!

Extracts from the audio available at <https://www.youtube.com/watch?v=LyTE-1DGxnE>. Accessed on April 12, 2019.

Chapter 8

Track 21 — Page 107

Ben, 8

Go on the computer. I play video games, I go in the garden, I do reading, writing, cooking... I quite like cooking cakes and things, and I've won a cake competition in my school... It was a lemon cake.

Taylor, 11

I like to go and play out with my friends and that [*sic*] and talk to them a lot.

Rishi, 11

I like to play badminton in the garden. I don't get the chance to do badminton much. But it's really nice to play badminton.

Daniel, 12

I like art, I like playing football and I like going out with my mates. I like football 'cause it's really fun, and we get lots of competitions... And I like art because I find it really creative.

Philipa, 11

I play the flute and... I go to Drama and... I like to go swimming.

Extracts from the audios available at <https://www.youtube.com/watch?v=YUii2oIgCDM>; <https://www.youtube.com/watch?v=6NHkCRgmbUI>. Accessed on May 10, 2019.

Glossary

CHAPTER 1

A
advantage: vantagem
adventure: aventura
against: contra
age: idade
audience: público
avoid: evitar

B
background: formação, experiência
beginning: início
believe: acreditar
belong: pertencer
both: ambos/as
brainstorm: fazer tempestade de ideias

C
character: personagem
choose: escolher
classmate: colega de classe
clear: claro/a
clothes: roupas
colony: colônia
constantly: constantemente
contestant: competidor/a, participante
country: país

D
daily: diário/a
disadvantage: desvantagem
distort: distorcer
draft: escrever rascunho
draw: desenhar

E
easy: fácil
entertainment: entretenimento
entry: verbete
everywhere: em todos os lugares
exit: saída

F
find: encontrar
foreigner: estrangeiro/a
found: encontrado/a

G
goal: objetivo

H
hear: ouvir
hyphen: hífen

I
inspirer: inspiração, quem ou o que inspira

L
letter: letra
lexicographer: lexicógrafo/a
life: vida
listen: escutar
look around: olhar, inspecionar

M
magazine: revista
meaning: significado
mention: mencionar
movie: filme

N
normally: normalmente
noun: substantivo

P
place: local
possess: possuir
presenter: apresentador/a
pronoun: pronome

Q
quantity: quantidade
quick: rápido/a

R
rather than: em vez de
recognize: reconhecer
role-play: encenar

S
same: mesmo/a
sentence: frase
share: compartilhar
sign: placa
skill: habilidade
social networking service: serviço de redes sociais
spell: soletrar
spelling bee: concurso de soletração
standby: modo de espera
subway: metrô

T
target audience: público-alvo
thesaurus: dicionário de sinônimos
together: juntos/as
translator: tradutor/a
twice: duas vezes
type: tipo

U
understand: compreender
unknown: desconhecido/a

V
volunteer: voluntário/a

W
watch: assistir a
way: caminho; forma, maneira
welcome: bem-vindo/a
word: palavra
wrong: incorreto/a

CHAPTER 2

A
a bit: um pouco
add: adicionar, acrescentar
again: novamente
appear: aparecer
appearance: aparência
available: disponível

B
back: fundo
between: entre
birth: nascimento
blank: em branco

C
change: mudar
chart: tabela
child: criança
clearly: claramente
contracted: contraído/a, abreviado/a
creature: criatura
cross out: riscar
cutting: recorte

D
deduction: dedução
depicted: retratado/a, representado/a
detail: detalhe
done: feito/a
driver's license: carteira de habilitação

E
extract: trecho
eye: olho

F
feel: sentir
fill in: preencher
flag: bandeira
funny: engraçado/a

G
give: dar
goalkeeper: goleiro/a
grab (someone's) attention: atrair a atenção (de alguém)
grade: série, ano escolar
guess: adivinhar

H
happen: acontecer
horse(back) riding: andar a cavalo

I
introduce oneself: apresentar-se
invite: convidar

K
kind: tipo
know: saber, conhecer

L
lab: laboratório
left: esquerda
look for: procurar
luck: sorte

M
make up: formar
match: associar, relacionar; partida, jogo
meet: encontrar
missing: ausente, faltante

N
news: notícia
newspaper: jornal
next to: ao lado de
nickname: apelido
novel: romance (livro)

O
other: outro/a

P
period: ponto-final
photo caption: legenda de foto
pose: posar
press conference: coletiva de imprensa
proud: orgulhoso/a
provide: fornecer
put: colocar

R
reader: leitor/a
ready: pronto/a
reflect: refletir
right: direita
rock: arrasar (coloquial)
rule: regra

S
sailing: velejar
scene: cena
second: segundo/a
self-introduction: autoapresentação
short: curto/a
show: mostrar
small: pequeno/a
soccer: futebol
son: filho
sound: parecer, soar
speaker: falante
stay: permanecer
stick: colar
subject: sujeito
successful: bem-sucedido/a
suppose: supor, imaginar
surname: sobrenome
swimming: natação

T
tag: marcador
talk: conversar, falar
team: time
troublesome: encrenqueiro/a

U
uncomfortable: desconfortável
useful: útil

W
Well done!: Bom trabalho!
whenever: sempre que

CHAPTER 3

A
a lot: muito/a
able: apto/a, capaz
adopted: adotado/a
also: também
amuse: divertir
apply: aplicar
argue: discutir
aunt: tia
awareness: consciência

B
birthplace: local de nascimento
brother: irmão

C
canvas: tela (de pintura)
chore: afazer, tarefa doméstica
clockwise: sentido horário
comedian: comediante
comic strip: tirinha (de quadrinhos)
conduct: conduzir
convey: transmitir
cook: cozinhar
cousin: primo/a
cute: fofinho/a

D
daughter: filha
donation: doação

F
father: pai
father-in-law: sogro
floor: chão

G
grandfather: avô
grandmother: avó

H
half-brother: meio-irmão
hate: odiar
have fun: divertir-se
health: saúde
highlighted: destacado/a
household: doméstico/a
husband: esposo

I
in order to: a fim de
interview: entrevistar; entrevista

L
label: rotular
look: parecer
look after: cuidar de
look at: observar
luckily: por sorte
lunch: almoço

M
main: principal
mind: mente
mother: mãe
mother-in-law: sogra

N
near: perto

O
only child: filho/a único/a

P
pack: fazer a mala
panel: quadro
parent: pai/mãe
plot: enredo, trama
potato chip: batata frita (em formato de salgadinho)
pregnancy: gravidez
pressure: pressão
pride: orgulho
private: particular

Q
quarrel: discutir, brigar

R
refer: referir-se
relationship: relacionamento
role: papel, função

S
scatter plot: diagrama de dispersão

screenwriter: roteirista
secondary: secundário/a
sheet: folha (de papel)
sibling: irmão/irmã
sister: irmã
sketch: esboço, rascunho
someone: alguém
speech bubble: balão de fala
spend time: passar um tempo
strange: estranho/a
stuff: coisas
Sure!: Claro!

T
teen: adolescente
teenager: adolescente
thought: pensamento
trip: viagem
TV set: aparelho de televisão

U
uncle: tio

W
watercolor: aquarela
weekend: fim de semana
wife: esposa
woman: mulher

CHAPTER 4

A
above: acima
abroad: no exterior
assignment: tarefa
attendance: frequência, comparecimento

B
based on: baseado/a em
below: abaixo
break: intervalo, recreio

C
class: aula; classe
classify: classificar
classroom: sala de aula
colorful: colorido/a
content: conteúdo
cow: vaca
crowded: lotado/a

D
dismissal: dispensa
do: fazer
Drama: Teatro

E
ESL (English as a second language): inglês como segunda língua

F
focus: focar
freedom: liberdade
French: Francês
Friday: sexta-feira

G
gesture: gesto
go: ir
grid: grade
guide: guia

H
have: ter
holiday: feriado
homeroom: horário de chamada
homeschooling: ensino domiciliar

I
improve: melhorar

L
learn: aprender
lesson: aula
library: biblioteca
live: morar
lonely: solitário/a

M
midday: meio-dia
milk: ordenhar
Monday: segunda-feira

N
named: chamado/a
next: próximo/a
non-profit: sem fins lucrativos
notice board: quadro de avisos

O
open: aberto/a
outcome: resultado

P
Physical Education (PE): Educação Física
Physics: Física
poetry: poesia
preferably: preferencialmente
previous: anterior

R
reason: razão, motivo
recess: intervalo
refugee: refugiado/a
rehearse: ensaiar
report card: boletim escolar
resource: recurso
roll call: chamada

S
school subject: disciplina escolar
send: enviar, mandar
should: dever (ao fazer uma sugestão)
sign in: entrar
slower: mais devagar
Spanish: Espanhol
speak up: falar mais alto
survey: enquete, pesquisa

T
Thursday: quinta-feira
timetable: quadro de horários
Tuesday: terça-feira

W
wear: usar, vestir
Wednesday: quarta-feira
week: semana
welcome: receber alguém
world: mundo

CHAPTER 5

A
agree: concordar

B
be sure: ter certeza
become: tornar-se

C
can: poder, conseguir
certain: certo/a, determinado/a
clean: limpar; limpo/a
clear the table: tirar a mesa
collect: recolher

comic book: revista em quadrinhos
courage: coragem

D
dancer: dançarino/a
disagree: discordar
do the dishes: lavar a louça
do the laundry: lavar a roupa

E
either: também não
elderly: idosos
entertain: entreter
erase: apagar
everything: tudo

F
fear: medo
feed the pet: alimentar o animal de estimação
feeling: sentimento, sensação
frustrated: frustrado/a
fun: divertido/a

G
garden: jardim, horta
greet: cumprimentar

H
hard: difícil

I
insecurity: insegurança
interact: interagir

J
join: juntar-se a
joke: piada

L
laugh: rir
look up: procurar

M
make the bed: arrumar a cama
meal: refeição
money: dinheiro
month: mês
most: a maior parte de

N
neighbor: vizinho/a
neighborhood: bairro, vizinhança
never: nunca

O
often: com frequência
older: mais velho/a
once: uma vez

P
painting: quadro, pintura
parody: paródia
plan: planejar; plano
prejudice: preconceito

Q
quote: citação

R
rarely: raramente
record: gravar
reply: responder

S
school supply: material escolar
scream: grito
seldom: infrequente
selfish: egoísta
sense: noção
some: alguns/algumas

something: algo
sometimes: às vezes
sweep: varrer

T
take care: cuidar
take out the trash: levar o lixo para fora
teach: ensinar
text: texto; enviar mensagem de texto pelo celular
thing: coisa
think: pensar; achar, considerar
time: tempo; vez
truth: verdade
try: tentar, experimentar

U
usually: geralmente

W
walk the dog: levar o cachorro para passear
want: querer
water: regar (as plantas)
while: enquanto
who: quem

Y
year: ano
yet: ainda

CHAPTER 6

A
accent: sotaque
angry: irritado/a
application: solicitação
arrive: chegar

B
bar: barra
blocked: bloqueado/a
bump: bater
button: botão

C
check: assinalar; verificar
confuse: confundir
couch: sofá

F
fist bump: cumprimentar com um soquinho amigável
food: comida

G
get together: reunir-se, encontrar-se

H
Howdy? (abbr.)/How do you do?: Como vai?
Howzit goin? (abbr.)/How is it going?: Como vão as coisas?
hug: abraçar

L
later: mais tarde
laughter: risada
load: carregar
luggage: bagagem

M
make fun: ridicularizar
maybe: talvez

move: mudar-se

N
networking: interagindo (coloquial); rede de comunicação
nice: legal
nose: nariz

O
order: pedir

P
party: festa
people: pessoas; povo
physically: fisicamente
player: jogador/a
press: pressionar

Q
quickly: rapidamente
quit: abandonar, desistir

R
raise: subir, aumentar
require: exigir, requerer
roommate: colega de quarto

S
save: economizar; salvar
section: seção
shake hands: cumprimentar dando as mãos
show: apresentar, mostrar; programa de TV
sleep: dormir
spoken: falado/a
starring: estrelando
suitcase: mala
Sup? (abbr.)/What is up?: E aí?, Tudo bem?

T
take part in: participar de
tonight: hoje à noite
type: digitar; tipo

W
Whazzup? (abbr.)/What is up?: E aí?, Tudo bem?
where: onde
wish: desejar

CHAPTER 7

A
absent: ausente
adjustment: ajuste
advertising: propaganda
arm: braço

B
bat: bastão, taco
behavior: comportamento
board: tabuleiro
bounce: quicar a bola no chão

C
catch: pegar
cheat: trapacear
cool down: esfriar
cycling: ciclismo

D
development: desenvolvimento

F
fair: de maneira justa
finger: dedo
fitness: preparo físico
foot (pl. feet): pé (pés)
forget: esquecer
free: livre
friendship: amizade

H
head: cabeça
helmet: capacete
hit: bater, atingir

I
injured: machucado/a

J
jumping jack: polichinelo

K
kick: chutar

L
lead: liderar
leg: perna

N
neck: pescoço

P
peace: paz
price: preço
purpose: objetivo
push-up: flexão
put up: afixar

R
remember: lembrar
rope: corda
rubber: borracha
run: correr

S
safety: segurança
sample: amostra
sell: vender
sick: doente
sign up: inscrever-se
size: tamanho
skating: patinação
summary: resumo

T
take place: acontecer
tell: contar
thirsty: com sede
tip: dica

W
wait: esperar
warm up: aquecer

CHAPTER 8

A
alone: sozinho/a
amazingly: incrivelmente
ancient: antigo/a, desatualizado/a

B
baking: fazer bolos e doces
besides: além de
building: edifício, construção

C
channel: canal

commonly: comumente
criticism: crítica

D
diagnose: diagnosticar
disability: deficiência
disclaimer: ressalva

E
equally: igualmente
evil: mau/má

F
field: campo
find out: descobrir
flute: flauta
fly a kite: empinar pipa
follower: seguidor/a

G
glasses: óculos
go out: sair
grumpy: rabugento/a

H
hang: pendurar
hang out: passar o tempo livre
height: altura

I
indoor: em local fechado

L
launch: lançar
leisure: lazer

M
make work: fazer funcionar
marital status: estado civil
moon: lua

O
outdoor: ao ar livre
own: próprio/a

P
paint: pintar
pattern: padrão
perhaps: talvez

R
rest: descanso
river: rio
run: administrar

S
short: abreviação; curto/a
sing: cantar
smear: esfregar
spare: livre
strong: forte
sunset: pôr do sol

T
trait: traço, peculiaridade

U
underwater: debaixo d'água
untrained: destreinado/a

W
weight: peso
wheelchair: cadeira de rodas
whose: cujo/a

Y
yawn: bocejo; bocejar

Learning more

Capítulo 1

O inglês nosso de cada dia

O inglês nosso de cada dia. *Pé na rua,* São Paulo: TV Cultura, 25 de maio de 2009. Programa de TV.

Você já se perguntou por que utiliza termos como *fast food*, *OK*, *deletar*, *software,* entre outras palavras e expressões em inglês? No episódio "O inglês nosso de cada dia", os apresentadores do programa *Pé na Rua*, da TV Cultura, entrevistam jovens perguntando-lhes acerca do uso da língua inglesa no seu cotidiano. As entrevistas atestam que o inglês é utilizado nos mais diversos contextos de comunicação.

Capítulo 2

Where children sleep (James Mollison)

Na série de fotos intitulada *Where children sleep* (disponível *online*), o fotógrafo James Mollison traz imagens intrigantes mostrando crianças de diferentes países em seus quartos. Cada foto traz uma perspectiva que nos faz refletir sobre o que constitui a identidade de cada criança frente às condições em que ela vive e a cultura de seu país.

Capítulo 3

The Croods

Dirigido por Chris Sanders e Kirk DeMicco.
Estados Unidos: DreamWorks Animation, distribuído por Fox Films, 2013.

The Croods é uma animação que retrata o cotidiano de uma família pré-histórica que vive em uma caverna sob a liderança do pai, Grug (Father Grug). Grug é um personagem que incentiva a esposa e os filhos a não explorarem o novo, pois pode ser perigoso. No entanto, quando a caverna (e morada) da família é destruída, os *Croods* precisam desbravar o mundo para encontrar outro lugar para viver. Dessa forma, a família precisa aprender a se manter unida perante uma situação desafiadora.

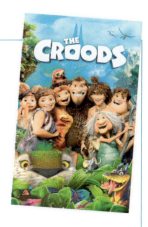

Capítulo 4

Confessions of a Former Bully

Escrito por Trudy Ludwig.
New York: Dragonfly Books, 2012.

O livro *Confessions of a Former Bully* conta a história de Katie, uma garota que pratica *bullying* na escola e é chamada para comparecer à diretoria.
A personagem é questionada sobre seu comportamento em relação aos/às colegas que ofendeu e passa a refletir sobre suas atitudes. Trata-se de um livro cuja voz é da própria praticante de *bullying*; por isso, a obra introduz uma perspectiva diferente e instigante sobre o *bullying* na escola.

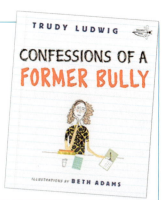

Capítulo 5

Explorando obras de arte: *Mona Lisa* e *O Grito*

Para saber mais sobre as obras *Mona Lisa* e *O Grito*, presentes no capítulo, acesse a internet e faça uma busca, respectivamente, pelo Museu do Louvre (Paris, França) e pela Galeria Nacional (Oslo, Noruega). Ambos os museus exibem partes de seus acervos e trazem informações sobre essas e muitas outras obras.

Capítulo 6

The Emoji Movie

Dirigido por Tony Leondis.
Estados Unidos: Sony Pictures Animation, 2017.

Na cidade de Textopolis, escondida no celular de um garoto chamado Alex, habitam os *emojis*, cada qual com uma expressão facial própria. No entanto, Gene é um *emoji* que tem múltiplas expressões e demonstra diversos sentimentos. Determinado a ser como os demais, Gene segue em uma busca e tem que passar por vários aplicativos antes que o celular de Alex seja apagado.

Capítulo 7

Kid Athletes: True Tales of Childhood from Sports Legends

Escrito por David Stabler.
Philadelphia, PA: Quirk Productions, 2015.

Kid Athletes é um livro que apresenta 20 histórias sobre a infância de atletas bem-sucedidos da atualidade. A narrativa mostra as barreiras que essas personalidades tiveram que transpor para que hoje chegassem onde estão.

Capítulo 8

Diary of a Wimpy Kid

Escrito por Jeff Kinney.
New York: Amulet Books, 2007.

Diary of a Wimpy Kid é uma série de livros cuja história é contada por Greg Heffley, um garoto que ingressa no Ensino Fundamental II. Decidido a documentar o que se passa na sua vida, o garoto começa a escrever em um diário, contando as situações que vivencia na escola e em casa. Os livros trazem as próprias anotações e desenhos de Greg, ilustrando as aventuras e peripécias de seu dia a dia.

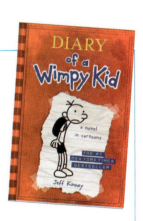

Track list

Track	Chapter	Activity	Page
1	Introduction	-	-
2	1	2	15
3	1	4	15
4	1	2, 3	16
5	1	4	17
6	1	5	17
7	2	2	26
8	2	2, 3	29
9	2	4	29
10	2	5	29
11	3	2	43
12	3	3	43
13	4	2	55
14	4	3	55
15	4	4	55
16	5	3, 4, 5, 6	69
17	6	2, 3	81
18	7	1	91
19	7	3	92
20	7	2, 3	95
21	8	3, 4	107

References

HOUAISS, Antonio. (Ed.). *Webster's Dicionário Inglês-Português.* Rio de Janeiro: Record, 1998. p. 874.

MATHEWS-AYDINLI, Julie (Ed.). *International Education Exchanges and Intercultural Understanding:* Promoting Peace and Global Relations. Ankara: Palgrave Macmillan, 2017.

WALDER, Chaim. *Kids Speak: Children Talk about Themselves.* New York: Feldheim Publishers, 1994. p. 13.

WALDER, Chaim. *Kids Speak 3: Children Talk about Themselves.* New York: Feldheim Publishers, 1997. p. 37.